BY JOE PAPRO, AND JULIANNE STANZ

THE CATECHIST'S BACKPACK

SPIRITUAL ESSENTIALS FOR THE JOURNEY

LOYOLA PRESS.
A JESUIT MINISTRY
Chicago

LOYOLA PRESS.
A JESUIT MINISTRY

3441 N. Ashland Avenue
Chicago, Illinois 60657
(800) 621-1008
www.loyolapress.com

Cover and interior design by Loyola Press
Cover art credit: Backpack, Ryan McVay/Photodisc/Thinkstock, shoes, epantha/iStock/Thinkstock

ISBN-13: 978-0-8294-4246-5
ISBN-10: 0-8294-4246-4
Library of Congress Control Number: 2014955517

Printed in the United States of America
15 16 17 18 19 20 RRD/USA 10 9 8 7 6 5 4 3 2

DEDICATION

Dedicated to the memory of Lee Nagel, a master catechist who spiritually filled the backpacks of so many with his lively stories, booming laughter and infectious sense of joy.

Other Loyola Press books by Joe Paprocki

*The Catechist's Toolbox: How to Thrive
as a Religious Education Teacher*

*A Well-Built Faith: A Catholic's Guide to
Knowing and Sharing What We Believe*

*The Bible Blueprint: A Catholic's Guide to
Understanding and Embracing God's Word*

*Living the Mass: How One Hour a Week Can
Change Your Life (with Fr. Dominic Grassi)*

*Practice Makes Catholic: Moving from
a Learned Faith to a Lived Faith*

*Beyond the Catechist's Toolbox: Catechesis That
Not Only Informs but Also Transforms*

*7 Keys to Spiritual Wellness: Enriching Your Faith
by Strengthening the Health of Your Soul*

*Under the Influence of Jesus: The Transforming
Experience of Encountering Christ*

CONTENTS

Acknowledgments

I would like to thank the following people: Arlene Astrowski and Deb Breakey, two excellent catechetical leaders, who allowed me to practice my catechetical craft at their respective parishes for a number of years; Maureen, my spiritual director, for supplying me with what I need for my spiritual backpack; Doug Hall for his wonderful cartoons; my wife, Jo, and my kids, Mike and Amy, for their nurturing love.

Joe Paprocki

To the many catechetical leaders, especially those in the Diocese of Green Bay, who mentor and encourage me: thank you for your guidance and patience. To the family and friends who support and nourish me: thank you for your help and kindness. To my rock, my husband Wayne, for his unwavering confidence in me and for his dedication to our family: thank you for your love.

Julianne Stanz

Introduction

Catechists must have a deep spirituality, i.e. they must live in the Spirit, who will help them to renew themselves continually in their specific identity.   —*Guide for Catechists*, no. 6

Backpacking is a fun, healthy, and physically challenging way to enjoy a journey of discovery. Setting off on a new adventure can bring all sorts of surprises, opportunities, and challenges. Through the journey itself, we acquire new insights and deeper understanding, and we often arrive at our destination energized and strengthened. Of course, anyone setting forth on a backpacking journey knows that there are many things to take into consideration and certain necessities that need to be packed. You have to choose a location and take into account its geography and inherent dangers. You need to bring along a compass, GPS, or maps; a water supply; first aid kit; proper clothing and footwear; nutritional and nonperishable foods; personal hygiene items; supplies and equipment; and sunscreen and bug spray. All these items can help ensure that your journey will be as fulfilling and enjoyable as possible.

In a similar way, catechists are engaged in a stimulating and challenging faith journey of discovery. Without the proper essentials for this spiritual journey, a catechist can run the risk of encountering fatigue, obstacles, frustrations, and even danger, all of which threaten to reduce the enjoyment and fulfillment of the journey or possibly cut it short. Suffice it to say, catechists require certain spiritual resources that enable them not only to endure the journey but to thrive on it.

"After three weeks of enjoying the church's services, prayer, fellowship, and counseling, I still feel a deep spiritual yearning. So I'm going to sue your socks off."

This means that, in addition to acquiring teaching techniques, learning strategies, and sharpening methodologies, we must also be tending to our spirituality. As catechists, we are not teachers of a subject, but rather witnesses to a living person: Jesus Christ. As such, we are called to cultivate that relationship and to share that relationship with others. These actions—both the cultivation and the sharing of our relationship with Christ—make up our spirituality.

What Is Spirituality?

In general, spirituality refers to how humans experience and nurture their relationship with God. Every human being has a spirituality. Christian spirituality relates to God in and through Jesus Christ. When it is actively pursued, spirituality is a path to holiness. Now, while the spiritual lives of all Christians share certain characteristics, a person's particular spirituality is unique. It is influenced by the person's education, formation, gender, geographical location, age, ethnic background, and so on. Thus we can speak of spiritualities that are Celtic, Ignatian, Dominican, Hispanic, and pre-Vatican II, just to name a few. By the same token, a person's spirituality is influenced by his or her vocation or state in life. A married person has a different spirituality than a celibate priest or nun. A single person's spiritual life expresses itself differently than that of a married person. So to some extent, every person's spirituality is unique because each of us is a unique human being.

With that in mind, we can talk about the spirituality of the catechist. When we speak of catechists in this book, we are referring to all those who facilitate faith formation with children, youth, young adults, or adults in general. Did you know that being a catechist is a vocation? The word *vocation* comes from the Latin word *vocatio*, meaning "to call" or "to summon." The summons to be a catechist is no less than a call or a summons from God! It's possible that you have not considered this. Few of us have experienced an epiphany that caused us to go to our parish one day and declare that God has called us to be a catechist. Many of us came into the ministry of catechesis through an unexpected conversation, phone call, or e-mail. But God often speaks to us in unique ways—which is why it makes perfect sense that catechists are called to develop a spirituality that's unique to catechists.

I Couldn't Believe It!

Christine's three children were in middle school religious education. She often engaged the director of religious education, Anne, in conversation about what her children were learning in class and how they were talking about this at home. One day Anne asked Christine to be a catechist. "I couldn't believe it," Christine said, "I felt so honored and humbled that Anne, whom I trusted and admired, would think I was capable of passing along my faith to others. At first I said no, but the more I thought about it, the more excited I became. If it wasn't for Anne seeing something special in me, I would never have considered that I had the necessary gifts for becoming a catechist.

–Julianne

Christine's story is familiar to many of us. Some of us were asked by a pastor, a parish catechetical leader, or one of our children to consider helping out in a parish faith formation program. These people recognized in us the potential and the gifts necessary to be a catechist, even if we ourselves had yet to recognize them. Wanting to be of service, we agreed—perhaps tentatively at first. We took a leap of faith because we trusted the person who asked us to be of service. But then, somehow, our one-year commitment became two, and two years grew into five.

Somewhere along the way we realized that we loved sharing our faith with those we serve. We realized that in preparing for our classes we were growing in our understanding and love of Jesus Christ and the church. These were possibly the first stirrings of our vocation as catechists.

> If I say, "I will not mention him, or speak any more in his name," then within me there is something like a burning fire shut up in my bones; I am weary with holding it in, and I cannot.
>
> —JEREMIAH 20:9

Six Non-Negotiables

Because of our vocation, we catechists are called to embark on a unique spiritual journey. In order to thrive on this journey, we need to carry some key spiritual resources in our catechist's backpack. These spiritual resources are identified and explored in the *Guide for Catechists* (1993). This document, issued by the Vatican office called the Congregation for the Evangelization of Peoples, describes the spirituality of the catechist, which is grounded in the spirituality of the laity and flows from the sacrament of baptism. In a nutshell, a catechist's spirituality is marked by these six characteristics:

1. Openness to God
2. Openness to the church
3. Openness to the world
4. Authenticity of life
5. Missionary zeal
6. Devotion to Mary

These six characteristics serve as the focus of this book. To show how each one is essential for the catechist's journey, we compare it to an item that is essential for backpacking. Here is a quick look at these items for the journey.

➕ **Radical Reliance on God: An Abundant Supply of Water** Every backpacker knows that without water, a person cannot survive. Water is the source of life and the most essential resource to include in one's backpack. Catechists, likewise, recognize their spiritual source of life: God! The spiritual journey is sustained primarily by an abundant supply of Living Water—God's own life within us. Catechists are called to a radical reliance on God and learn to quench their thirst for God on a daily basis. This is a reliance on a *living* Word—a person—whom we recognize as the source of all life. We desire deeply to enter into intimacy with God and to invite others to do the same. Our desire is to be transformed by this life-giving relationship and to invite others to this saving and sustaining transformation.

> We desire deeply to enter into intimacy with God and to invite others to do the same.

➕ **Commitment to the Church: Adequate Food and Shelter** In order to be sustained on the journey, a backpacker needs an adequate supply of nutritional food as well as the tools and utensils needed to prepare that food. Our call to serve as catechists comes from the church, which is the source of our nourishment and provides us with the tools we need to access that nourishment and to share it with others. We're not self-reliant; we are sent on a mission and nourished along the way by the church. Having been called to serve as catechists, we're nourished by the church and empowered to bring that nourishment to others.

➕ **Openness to the World: A Topographical Map**   When backpacking, it's helpful to have a topographical map, a field guide, or a navigational system that familiarizes hikers with the geography and terrain they are about to traverse. It helps to know about wildlife and plant life in the area as well as opportunities and dangers that may be encountered along the way. As catechists, we need to familiarize ourselves with the "terrain" of this world. The Holy Spirit was poured forth so that we could proclaim the gospel to all nations. This serves as our map, compass, and ultimately our "GPSS"—our global positioning spiritual system. Without such a tool we would wander aimlessly, without direction. With it, we can stay in touch with the field in which the seeds of the gospel are to be sown: the world. We are called, however, not simply to immerse ourselves in the world but to survey it, engage it, and challenge it so that it may be transformed in and through Christ.

➕ **Consistency and Authenticity: The Right Clothing and Footwear** Few things can ruin a backpacking adventure like inadequate clothing and footwear can. In order to withstand the elements, navigate difficult terrain, and maintain a good pace, a backpacker needs appropri-

> **Being a catechist is not a hat that we put on and take off as we please.**

ate clothing and sturdy, supportive shoes. This is no time to "make do" with your old sneakers and T-shirts. You want gear that's made for the job! As catechists, too, we need the proper attire to withstand life's ever-changing terrain. In this case, the proper attire is our true being, which is Christ himself. By virtue of our baptism, we have "put on" Christ and become a member of his body. In other words, being a catechist is not a hat that we put on and take off as we please. We are not teachers of a subject or a skill that pertains to one area of our lives. Instead, we invite others into a way of life that defines who we are at our very core. The simple fact is, we can't teach what (or who) we don't know. This means that we have to strive to know Jesus authentically, to internalize his message, and to follow the Catholic way of life that leads to him. We need to be the real deal.

✚ **Missionary Zeal: Fuel and Matches**   Along the journey, a backpacker may need to start a fire for cooking, keeping warm, or both. In order to do so, he or she needs matches to start the fire and a reliable source of fuel to keep it burning. Similarly, the vocation of the catechist calls us to be "on fire" for Christ. Our desire to share Christ with others is powerful and sometimes overwhelming. We can't help but share the gospel with others! In addition to this powerful flame, we also need staying power, a missionary zeal that is fueled by an infinitely reliable source. This fuel is the Holy Spirit.

✚ **Devotion to Mary and the Saints: Flashlight and Batteries**   At times, it may grow so dark along the path or at the campsite that a backpacker needs to generate a little light with a reliable flashlight and fresh batteries. Catechists recognize that the spiritual path can sometimes grow murky, too. Luckily, we have reliable sources of light—Mary and the saints—who brighten the path to Jesus and make it visible so that we do not stumble or lose our way. Mary was the first teacher of Jesus and the first disciple. She is a "living catechism" and a "model for catechists." The spirituality of all the baptized is enriched by devotion to Mary, but, as catechists, our ministry is especially enriched by devotion to the Blessed Mother and to all the saints who show us the way to the true Light of the World, Jesus Christ.

Anxious Parishioner: Father, people keep telling me to calm down. Can you recommend a retreat house where I can experience spiritual peace?
Pastor: Sure, but once YOU'RE there, I doubt that it will be peaceful any longer!

"Yes! My Calling!"

My fellow eighth-grade catechist, John, had been teaching for over ten years, starting when his daughters entered the program in first grade. Now that his youngest daughter was being confirmed, I asked John if he was coming back next year. He said, "I thought I was going to retire when the last of my girls was confirmed. But now, I realize that I want to come back and keep teaching. I think I've come to recognize that this is my . . . my . . ." "Calling?" I asked. "Yes! My calling!" he responded with excitement. John had not fully realized before now that what he was doing was a vocation.   –Joe

In each chapter of *The Catechist's Backpack*, we'll delve more deeply into one of these items for the journey, reflect on it, and apply it to our own lives and our own vocation as catechists. These six characteristics encapsulate what all catechists have or seek to have in our relationship with God, through Jesus Christ, in the Holy Spirit. Just as a backpacker needs essential resources, a healthy spiritual life also requires essential resources. Because it's true that you can't give what you don't have, catechists need these spiritual resources if we hope to share them with others and prepare them for the journey.

An Unquenchable Thirst for Living Water

Many of us would not describe ourselves as deeply spiritual. In fact, we often feel embarrassed that our spiritual life is not as strong as we'd like it to be. If you feel as though you hunger for God and desire to know him better, consider yourself blessed! This is the foundation of a healthy spiritual life—not a sense of completeness or perfection, but an unquenchable thirst for Living Water. Among Jesus' last words on the cross were "I am thirsty" (John 9:28). Jesus' cry for living water was not just a cry for physical relief from the dehydration he was experiencing.

> **"What you are is God's gift to you, what you become is your gift to God."**
> —Hans Urs von Balthasar

It was also a cry to quench the thirst of our desires and our longings—ultimately, a cry for our salvation.

This thirst for Living Water is a thirst for God's very life, a longing for God that only God can satisfy. To thirst for God is natural and healthy—much healthier than taking God for granted or pretending not to thirst at all. To call out to God for help is not to show weakness. It is to acknowledge our relationship with God and our dependence on him. Even expressing anger with God is healthy because we only become angry with something we are invested in and care deeply about. The six characteristics of the catechist's spirituality are six ways we can deepen and broaden our investment in God and satisfy our thirst for him.

> Let the one who believes in me drink. As the scripture has said, "Out of his heart will flow rivers of living water."
> —JOHN 7:38

This book will help nurture your vocation as a catechist and nourish your spiritual life. You can use this book in a variety of ways. You may want to use it for personal reflection, or you might join or form a group at your parish and meet for weekly discussion and faith sharing. You might also pass the book along to a friend, especially one whom you feel would make a good catechist. However you use it, our hope is that this book will assist you in paying attention to the movements of God in your life and in cultivating your relationship with the Living God—which in turn will help you walk the journey with enthusiasm and authenticity and invite others to do the same.

What Catechists Are Saying about Their Spiritual Lives

❝My spiritual life right now can best be described by comparing it to the disciples waiting in the upper room for the Holy Spirit to come. I'm learning to rely on the Holy Spirit to take care of things that make me nervous! And the Holy Spirit is teaching me to trust. My favorite quote is by St. Catherine of Siena: "Be who God meant you to be and you will set the world on fire."

—Jenn

My spiritual life right now can best be described by comparing it to the journey of St Paul. He worked so hard to try and complete the divine plan of evangelization; he is an inspiration to me. I have to mention all of the help I received from the patron saint of catechists, St. John Bosco, for the past nine years; he has taught me patience and persistence. I feel I have been blessed to have had the chance to touch the spiritual lives of over 100 of God's children. *—Tony*

Presently my faith journey can be compared to Lent. There is desert wandering and dryness of spirit. The first demands a compass and the second needs to have thirst quenched. *—Susan*

My spiritual life right now can best be described by comparing it to the Samaritan woman in the Gospel of John, who meets Jesus at the well. Jesus reveals himself to her at the well, and every year he reveals himself to me. After my first class, I feel like the Samaritan woman after her talk with Jesus: I want to go out and tell everyone that I have met the Savior! *—Patty*

I am currently a catechist for a girl I have been with since she started the program at age three. . . . We will be entering the eighth grade this fall. She has cerebral palsy and does not communicate . . . except through her beautiful eyes. My experience these past years has been different than most. . . . I see Jesus in her every time we are together. . . . My spirituality can best be described by my Confirmation name, Marie. . . . I love Our Lady and want to do everything our Lord asks of me. *—Karen*

I have been a catechist for more than fifty years. My spiritual growth is somewhere between nascent and getting ready for the end. I am addicted to teaching and see my mentor as Paul, my patron. My prayer life is centered in the Liturgy of the Hours. *—Al*

I would describe my spiritual life as a catechist as being in a dormant winter phase right now. In adult faith formation I tend so much to the spiritual life of other adults, especially during Lent and Advent, that I often forget to minister to myself. But I know that winter is followed by spring and that the seeds that are germinating in the winter of my heart will bear fruit with rest, prayer, and the grace of God. I am strengthened by the time I take to pray the rosary daily in my car on the way to work. *—Penny*

It is only in the last few years that I have gotten comfortable with my own spiritual life and how it is expressed. In past years, I would have described myself as a spiritual seeker and found myself praying for my personality to be more of a steady and peaceful one rather than the strong and energetic one that I was given. I had an image in my head of a deeply spiritual person as a person who is calm, steady, serious, and soft-spoken. Definitely not me! I even knew someone who emulated the characteristics perfectly and so found myself praying to God to be just like this person! I realized one day, though, that God had given me a natural energy and strength of character that came from him. I could be a prayerful and spiritual person in my own way by thanking God for the gifts that he had given me, putting them to work for his purposes, and asking for God to increase the gifts that I had been given. **" "**

—Shaun

Chapter 1

Radical Reliance on God: An Abundant Supply of Water

Catechists should allow themselves to be drawn into the circle of the Father, who communicates the word; of the Son, the incarnate Word, who speaks only the words He hears from the Father; and of the Holy Spirit, who enlightens the mind to help it understand God's words and opens the heart to receive them with love and put them into practice.

—Guide for Catechists, no. 7

An Abundant Supply of Drinking Water

It's no secret that water is necessary for survival. No resource is more important for the well-being of a backpacker than an abundant water supply. In order to avoid dehydration, a backpacker needs to drink anywhere from two to eight liters, depending on the terrain and the temperature. And, although natural waters in streams and rivers along the journey might look pure and refreshing, they may contain harmful contaminants. These contaminants are not always obvious to us, so it is even more important that our drinking water come from a source which is pure and life-giving.

In order to survive and thrive on the catechist's journey, we rely on a pure source of Living Water: the very life of God that courses through our being and sustains us at all times. We may find ourselves tempted by other sources of "sustenance" that look appealing;

> **Everyone who thirsts, come to the waters.**
> —ISAIAH 55:1

however, like stream water, these may contain "contaminants" that cause more harm than good. Catechists recognize that our hearts yearn for the pure goodness of God "as a deer longs for flowing streams" (Psalm 42:1). To be a catechist is to be rooted in God: Father, Son, and Holy Spirit. Let's take a closer look at what it means to live with a radical reliance on God.

Trust Me

Two of the most frightening words in the English language are *trust me*. When someone uses these words, we are reminded of our own doubts and vulnerability. We know we are being asked to set aside our sense of self-direction

> ## Trust Springs from the Soul
>
> The Trinity and the shamrock were symbols that had great significance to the ancient Celtic people, among whom were the biblical Galatians. St. Patrick is said to have used the symbol of the shamrock to preach the gospel to the Irish by comparing its three leaves with the Father, the Son, and the Holy Spirit. This probably derived from the Celtic belief that trust springs from the soul, belief wells up from the heart, and faith comes from the mind.

and self-determination in order to let another guide us. In an instant, all our memories of broken trust seem to surface out of nowhere, begging the question, "Will this time be different?" To move forward, we must have faith in the person asking for our trust. We must place our well-being, our very heart, in that person's hands.

In the catechist's journey and in the journey of all the baptized, it is God who is saying, "Trust me." To do this takes both courage and faith. The catechist's faith is not merely an intellectual assent to a set of doctrines. It is the opening of our hearts and the giving of ourselves to another—in this case, to God.

A Journey of about Eighteen Inches

It has been said that the greatest journey that we will make as Christians is a journey of about eighteen inches. This is the approximate distance from our head to our heart. The Christian life is about translating what we know about God into a heartfelt response to him and to the world around us.

When we pray the Creed—"I believe in one God, the Father almighty. . . . in one Lord, Jesus Christ, the only Begotten Son of God . . . in the Holy Spirit, the Lord, the giver of life"—we are saying that we give our hearts to God—Father, Son, and Holy Spirit.

Trust does not come easily for many people. Many of us have experienced the loss of trust in our relationships. We feel broken, angry, vulnerable, and sensitive. We may say to ourselves that we will never trust again. When you give your heart to someone and he or she breaks it, it's certainly not easy to trust again. We can see the effects of broken trust in the children, youth, and adults we teach. We see it, too, in the families we interact with, including our own.

Trust is the foundation of faith, for it leads to hope. As catechists, we are called to a deep trust in God—an openness to entering into relationship with the Trinity: Father, Son, and Holy Spirit. This in turn gives us a great sense of hope. The Risen Christ, who came to us so intimately in the form of an innocent child, has given us the promise of eternal life.

> **Trust is the foundation of faith, for it leads to hope.**

Authentic trust in God touches us at the deepest core of our lives. It shapes who we are. It informs our values, convictions, decisions, and behaviors. As catechists, we become champions of the First Commandment; we are passionate about making God alone the center of our lives. This is what it means to live a God-centered life rather than an ego-centric one that places us at the center and God on the periphery. When God is our center, we model what that looks like for those we teach. We exert great energy to raise awareness of the many contaminated streams of water they may encounter: fame, power, pleasure, possessions, status, comfort, and so

Who Do You Trust Most?

I was teaching a group of eighth graders a class on placing our trust in God. I asked the students whom they trusted most. They gave a variety of answers: my mom, my dad, my sister, my brother, my best friend. But one young man very calmly responded: "me." He didn't feel he could trust anyone but himself. We've probably all had moments when we've felt very much the same way.   —Joe on. We see it as our mission to invite them to experience how God alone quenches the thirst within us. We do this because we ourselves have come to know and believe that this is true. And yet we, too, need to be reminded of this over and over again. Temptation is often quite subtle and never far away. We need to renew our radical reliance on God and continually rediscover for ourselves that God can and should be trusted.

"Do you have any references?"

Pope Francis has said that "the man or woman who has faith relies on God: entrusts himself or herself to Him! Trusting in God is what leads us to hope. Just as the confession of faith leads us to the worship and praise of God, so trust in God leads us to an attitude of hope. There are many Christians with a hope too watered down, not strong: a faint hope. Why? Because they do not have the strength and the courage to trust in the Lord."

As catechists, we are called to be mindful of our radical reliance on God—Father, Son, and Holy Spirit. How open am I to the love of the Father? How do I seek communion with Christ and experience his comforting presence? How do I allow myself to be molded by the Holy Spirit and transformed into a disciple of Christ? How am I growing as a courageous preacher of the Word, a champion of the First Commandment? Is my life marked by openness, joy, and hope? To nurture these qualities, we need to pray for faith—for trust—so that we can enter more deeply into the life-giving waters of the Trinity and live in relationship with God the Father, God the Son, and God the Holy Spirit.

To believe is to enter into relationship with another and to place our trust in that person. It is to have faith in what we cannot see. "Blessed are those who have not seen and yet have come to believe," Scripture tells us (John 20:29). At times, trust also requires that we risk our

> "Love God, serve God; everything is in that."
> —St. Clare of Assisi

I Know You Will Always Come Back

My son Ian, like most five-year-olds, is afraid of the dark. Usually his father or I have to lie down with him until he falls asleep. Before we go to sleep, one of us always checks on him and tucks his blankets around him. One night, when I returned to tuck Ian in, he opened his eyes and said, "It's okay, Momma, if you go away or sleep in your own bed because I know you always come back when I'm sleeping. That makes it easier for me to sleep, you know." And with that, he closed his eyes and fell fast asleep.   –Julianne

comfort, our reputation, and even our better judgment. Such trust is not easy! As catechists, we are convinced that our lives need to be centered in God. We probably have tried at various times to drink from other streams and, like St. Augustine, have come to believe that "our hearts are restless, Lord, until they find their rest in You." Like any other human being, however, we struggle with this. We need continuous reminders about where and in whom to place our trust. To keep focus, we practice radical reliance on God.

A Relationship of Self-Giving Love

To be radically reliant on God is to be open to a relationship with the Trinity—a relationship of self-giving love. All relationships involve trust, and to trust is risky. Perhaps the greatest risk of our lives is the risk of embracing our baptism—the everyday giving of our hearts to God, the entrusting of our lives to God, whom we cannot see. Thankfully, Scripture reminds us that God has proven worthy of that trust. This is what we teach our students—that God is trustworthy and gives us many reasons for hope.

> Trust in him at all times, O people; pour out your heart before him; God is a refuge for us.
> —Psalm 62:8

Waving to Jesus

When my daughter was three years old, she could be a bit of a challenge at Mass. Coming forward to receive Holy Communion, for example, was always interesting. She would accompany me and wave and smile at people and whisper little greetings to her friends along the way. One Sunday, as I was kneeling in prayer after communion, she asked me if Mass was almost over. I replied that very soon we would say good-bye to Jesus and go home. Very quietly she went out into the middle of the aisle, knelt down for a few moments, and then began to wave discreetly at the altar. After I managed to bring her back to the pew, I asked her whom she was saying good-bye to. "Jesus," she said. "I was making sure to say good-bye to him before we went home." It gladdened me to know that in my daughter's heart, Jesus is as real to her as the people she sees before her. Oh, that we would all approach Jesus with the same childlike simplicity and trust!

–Julianne

Catechesis: An Encounter with the Living Person of Jesus Christ

For many of those we teach, especially children, religious education is just one of many activities that make up a busy week. In their minds, faith formation gets lumped in with soccer, cheerleading, dance class, piano lessons, and football—and it will stay that way unless we invite our young people to meet a living person, Jesus Christ. Meeting and embracing Jesus is what transforms our efforts from teaching a subject to encountering a person. Through our own radical reliance on God—Father, Son, and Holy Spirit— we cultivate a spirituality that is alive and vibrant, enabling us to invite others to enter more deeply into this profound and life-changing relationship.

Questions for Reflection

As catechists, we want to make time on a regular basis to deepen our reliance on God: Father, Son, and Holy Spirit. We might pause daily or weekly to reflect on how God has shown through the events of our lives that he is worthy of our trust. Doing so will give us the conviction we need to teach others that placing their trust in God will not be in vain— and indeed, will bear fruit.

Here are a few questions you might use for reflection.

> Whom do you trust most in this world? Why? Who places trust in you?
> Identify a time when trust was broken in your life. How did (does) that affect you?
> Why do you personally believe that God can be trusted?
> How has your trust in God been validated or affirmed over the course of your life? This week? Today?
> If you are having difficulty trusting God, what may be causing that?
> In what situations do you find it most difficult to trust God? Easiest?
> What can you do to deepen your radical reliance on God?
> Who do you know who exhibits a radical reliance on God? What is it about this person that you would like to emulate?
> How does your reliance on God affect you in your role as a catechist?
> How do you recognize when you are spiritually thirsty? In what ways do you satisfy your thirst for the Living Waters of God?
> How can you help those you teach to be more reliant on God?
> Where do you feel the stirrings of hope in your heart as a catechist? How do you share that hope with those you teach?
> What would you let go of in order to feel really hopeful and trusting right now?

Margaret was a catechist seeking to deepen her knowledge of God, so she began attending a parish where the pastor was known for his profound theological knowledge. After the first homily, however, she found herself bored by the length and confused by the depth of his homilies. As she was leaving the church, the pastor cornered her and asked her what she thought of his homily. Not wishing to offend, she said, "Well, Father, it reminded me of the peace and love of God." She hoped to leave it at that, but the pastor pressed further. "Really?" he asked. "Why is that?" Margaret replied, "If you must know, Father, it reminded me of the peace of God because it passed all understanding and the love of God because it endured forever!"

For Further Reflection

"I invite all Christians, everywhere, at this very moment, to a renewed personal encounter with Jesus Christ, or at least an openness to letting him encounter them; I ask all of you to do this unfailingly each day."

—Pope Francis, *Evangelii Gaudium*

Spiritual Exercises

The following spiritual exercises are designed to deepen your radical reliance on God and to ensure that Living Waters are an essential element in your catechist's backpack. Consider sharing the fruits of your exercises with a friend or fellow catechist.

> Make time at the beginning of each day to give your heart to God. You can use your own words, or you might pray the *Suscipe* of St. Ignatius of Loyola.

> *Take, Lord, and receive all my liberty,*
> *my memory, my understanding*
> *and my entire will,*
> *all I have and call my own.*
> *You have given all to me.*
> *To You, Lord, I return it.*
> *Everything is yours; do with it what you will.*
> *Give me only your love and your grace,*
> *that is enough for me.*

> Radical reliance on God opens our hearts and minds to the possibilities around us. This, in turn, leads us to live in hope. Over the next several days, jot down in a journal or on an index card at least ten things that you are hoping for. Do so by completing this sentence:
> "I am hoping for/that . . ." Keep this list nearby so that you can glance at it frequently. Revise it occasionally. Before you begin to write your list, pray Psalm 62:1-8:

> *For God alone my soul waits in silence;*
> *from him comes my salvation.*
> *He alone is my rock and my salvation,*
> *my fortress; I shall never be shaken.*
> *How long will you assail a person,*
> *will you batter your victim, all of you,*
> *as you would a leaning wall, a tottering fence?*

Their only plan is to bring down a person of prominence.
They take pleasure in falsehood;
they bless with their mouths,
but inwardly they curse.
For God alone my soul waits in silence,
for my hope is from him.
He alone is my rock and my salvation,
my fortress; I shall not be shaken.
On God rests my deliverance and my honor;
my mighty rock, my refuge is in God.
Trust in him at all times, O people;
pour out your heart before him,
God is a refuge for us.

> Radical reliance on God is manifested in openness to others. In the days to come, make a specific plan to perform an out-of-the-ordinary act of hospitality that opens you up to another person or group of people. Perhaps you can identify someone around you in need of a special act of kindness. This act can be done at home, at work, or in your community. Spend a few moments afterward reflecting on your experience. What were you feeling before, during, and after your act of hospitality? Did anything surprise you? What was the hardest part of this act? What was the easiest? End your reflection by praying the Act of Love.

O Lord God, I love you above all things
and I love my neighbor for your sake
because you are the highest, infinite and perfect good,
worthy of all my love.
In this love I intend to live and die.   Amen.

> Radical reliance on God is fundamentally an attitude that informs our behaviors, choices, and way of life. It is tested, refined, and strengthened as we move forward on our journey. Take a moment to sit quietly and ponder this prayer in your heart. Notice where you feel called to pause and what feelings surface within you. For a few moments dwell in those feelings, and then conclude with a prayer of thanksgiving for God's faithfulness.

> Radical reliance on God involves a *metanoia*—a sincere conversion of heart and mind. As we turn toward God, we often turn away from something else. Take time to reflect on this idea. As you drink from

God's abundant well of love, mercy, and hope, remember also to identify patterns of sin that you have turned away from or wish to turn away from. Identify those "spiritual contaminants" that may have polluted your own well of love, mercy, and hope, and ask for forgiveness and the ability to reconcile those with God. If you have not been to the sacrament of reconciliation in some time, consider going again to talk about the issues that you have identified.

What Catechists Are Saying about Radical Reliance on God

"Little ones teach us about trust. Four-to-six-year-olds, generally, are not jaded or cynical with this life yet. They are so "full" of everything—life, wonderment, imagination, and most definitely trust. As adults, we tend to turn our backs on those people who disappoint us and break our trust. But that isn't so with little ones. They throw themselves right back at us and look for reasons to continue trusting us. We have so much to learn from them, don't we?　　　　　　　　　　　　　　　　　　　　　　　*–Ali*

I think we need to share our stories, with all the ups and downs, so that our young people can see real examples of how we've trusted God through everything in our lives. I think it's important for young people to see that unfortunate things do happen, but if we are people of faith, and trust in God, he will see us through the "bumps in the road."　　　　　*–Nancy*

I feel that I have evolved into a rather trusting person, and believe me, that is not always popular in the business world! I used to wake up in the night worrying about work, for example, but now I generally have become so trusting of God that I will just tell myself that Jesus will hold onto my work and life worries until morning and I go back to sleep.　　　　　*–Greg*

Trusting God is an ongoing journey for me. I try to practice what I call God-sightings every day: times when God is present in the everyday. This practice has helped me to trust God and share with others about his love and faithfulness to us. To be near God is good!　　　　　　　　　　*–Stephanie*

I do have an openness to the Father, Son, and Holy Spirit, and this is deepened every day by prayer and the work the Holy Spirit does for others through me. When I prepare before class, I open myself completely to let the Holy Spirit work through me.　　　　　　　　　　　　　*–Katherine*

Through the years, I have developed such a strong trust in God and his perfect love because I have personally seen evidence of it in my own life—in the circumstances of bringing my wife into my life, in the blessings he bestows on us on a daily basis, in how he has always found ways to get us through difficult times, and so on. The toughest thing I had to learn to do was to "Let go and let God," as in, "Let God show you the way." And that is a continual lifelong process of learning. *—Henry*

I agree that "trust" is the key word in growing closer to our Lord and in understanding God's ways over ours. Every time, I've basically said, "I don't know how, Lord, but I know you can. . . ." He has revealed answers to my prayers in ways I would never expect. I have seen God answer so many prayers, proving that when we place our worries, concerns, and needs in his hands, we are not forsaken. *—Nancy*

I heard someone say once that "If God brings you to it, then he will lead you through it." This has been a constantly unfolding revelation in my life. Because of this, I have a great sense of hope about God's plan for my life, even when I am not sure where I am going. I believe that the presence of God is with me in the smallest undertakings of my daily life and this provides comfort and strength even when I am afraid or feel alone. **"**

—Claire

Chapter 2

Commitment to the Church: Adequate Food and Shelter

As People of God and the Mystical Body of Christ, the Church requires from catechists a deep sense of belonging and responsibility, inasmuch as they are living and active members of it; as universal sacrament of salvation, it elicits the will to live its mystery and its manifold grace so as to be enriched by it and become a visible sign to the community. The catechist's service is never an individual or isolated act, but is always deeply ecclesial. —*Guide for Catechists*, no. 7

Sorry, No Motel

This is stating the obvious, of course, but backpacking takes place outdoors in the wilderness. This means that when it comes to eating and sleeping, a backpacker does not have (and does not seek) the luxury of checking into a motel for a warm meal and a soft bed. Part of the adventure of backpacking is getting back to basics, reconnecting with your need for peace and nature, and setting off on the road less traveled. In order to do this successfully, a backpacker must be sure to have an adequate supply of nutritional food and a tent for protection from the elements.

As catechists, where do our nutrition and shelter come from? Strictly speaking, of course, they come from God, but God "delivers" these realities to us through the church. Our unique call to serve as catechists comes from the church, and in turn for our service, the church offers us nourishment and shelter. As catechists, we are not "lone rangers"; we are sheltered and nourished in a very large tent, the church. But what is the church?

Here Is the Church, Here Is the Steeple

Children love a good nursery rhyme, and most adults can easily recall the nursery rhymes they were taught years ago. Here is one you may recall from your own childhood:

Here is the church.
Here is the steeple.
Open the doors and see all the people.
Close the doors and let them pray.
Open the doors and they've all gone away.

This nursery rhyme teaches us a simple truth: while we come to worship and give thanks to God in a physical building, the church is more than that. The church is also the people who are the body of Christ. It is not so much a place we go to as much as it is something we become. That something is not just a loose collection of like-minded individuals; rather, it is a living, breathing community of believers who are tethered, so to speak, to one another in faith and sheltered under the protection and love of the church.

Man Does Not Live by Air Alone!

A 1974 hit song by the Hollies exclaims, "All I need is the air that I breathe, yes to love you." While the sentiments in this song are delightful, man cannot, in fact, live by air alone. Food and shelter are also critical; if you go too long without either, your body will tell you.

We Are Church for Others

"When I first became a catechist, I went to church for myself and didn't think much about others. That was until the day I saw a young woman coming into church with four very young children. I knew that she had recently lost her husband tragically, and yet here she was sitting beside me with what must have been incredible sorrow in her heart. When it came time for the sign of peace, I found myself reaching out to her and saying, "Peace. I am so glad that you are here." Her smile through her tears touched my heart more than you could ever imagine. I realized then that we don't just go to church for ourselves but to "be" church to and for other people."   –Karen S.

A catechist realizes that because the journey we are on is long, it will require nutrition and shelter from a source beyond ourselves. Without these things, we will neither enjoy the journey nor have the wherewithal to meet the challenges it brings. Instead, we will find ourselves quickly drained and exhausted. We will lack the ability to focus productively on all that is happening around us. We will become miserable and focused on ourselves, self-absorbed and unable to see "the big picture." We will become consumed by what we lack rather than nourished by what we have.

Proper nutrition and shelter, on the other hand, keep us focused, energized, and on track. These essentials give us renewed energy, renewed perspective, and clear vision. They enable us to conquer life's mountains and pass through its valleys.

The food and shelter catechists need come from our relationship with the church because the vocation itself is rooted in our baptismal call. Our vocation is further strengthened in the sacraments of Eucharist and confirmation and nourished by the Holy Spirit. We cannot sustain ourselves in body and spirit without the food and shelter that the church gives us. Without it, we are weaker and more vulnerable as Christians. We lack the fervor and spirit not only to motivate and inspire ourselves, but also to motivate and inspire others.

> **We cannot sustain ourselves in body and spirit without the food and shelter that the church gives us.**

Sharing a Tent Is Not Easy

When I (Joe) was teaching in the high school seminary in Chicago some years ago, I recall talking to my students about the religious life and, in particular, explaining the evangelical counsels of poverty, chastity, and obedience. After a thorough explanation, I invited the students to ask questions or make comments. One young man said, "I don't know about this poverty, chastity, and obedience stuff. That seems pretty challenging. I think I'd rather get married."

Right. Go for the "easy life"!

I went on to explain that all baptized Christians are called to practice the spirit of these counsels—poverty, chastity, and obedience—which are the cornerstones of communal life. I explained that in marriage, we practice them in the following ways.

+ We practice **poverty** as a detachment from possessions. For example, parents do not hoard their possessions—their homes, furniture, cars, stereos, money, food—but share them with members of the family. Parents are constantly called to place the needs of their children above their own.

+ We practice **chastity** as faithfulness to one's sexuality. Married people recognize that the strength of the family rests on the strength of their committed and faithful relationship to each other as spouses.

+ We practice **obedience** as accountability. Family members do not come and go as they please but remain accountable to one another precisely out of love for one another.

In other words, the counsels remind us that we are members of a community, not isolated individuals. Today, in Western culture, individualism is worshiped. Through TV and other media, we are constantly told that we are our own best authority and that freedom to do as we please is the ultimate goal. In other words, no one can tell us what to do. No wonder so many of today's superheroes are loners: Batman, Iron Man, the Hulk—all today's versions of the Lone Ranger.

As catechists, though, we have a profound sense of community. We recognize that we are part of something bigger than ourselves. We are not inviting others to a "me and God" experience. We are inviting them to a "we and God" experience. The "my will

> **As catechists, we have a profound sense of community.**

be done" mindset, which characterizes so much of society, is replaced by a "thy will be done" attitude as we learn to place God and the needs of others before ourselves. We take great inspiration from men and women religious who live lives of poverty, chastity, and obedience, exemplifying for us that living in loving relationship with community is key to our salvation. The catechist's spirituality is characterized by a commitment to the community of the church and is nourished and sustained by that community.

Catechists Are Spiritual and Religious

You might have heard the expression "I am spiritual but not religious." Often what is at the heart of this sentiment is a desire for God but not for institutionalized religion. The word *religion* comes from the Latin word

A pig and a chicken stopped into a Catholic church just as the priest was delivering a homily about sharing with the community. The chicken said, "That's a good idea! Why don't we offer them some ham and eggs?" "Not so fast!" replied the pig. "For you, that's a contribution. For me, it's a total commitment!"

ligare, which means to "bind together." Being religious is not in conflict with the spiritual life. In fact, a truly integrated spiritual life is precisely one that is nourished and sheltered by the community of believers that we call the church. Religion and faith force us to come to grips with the reality that love of God and love of neighbor cannot be separated. It is within this church, filled with neighbors as imperfect as ourselves, that we learn to practice this love.

The church is the sacrament of union of all people with God. Once the doors of the church open at the end of Mass, we go forth into the world to share our love of Christ with others. We do so, however, fortified by an invisible reality forged by the Holy Spirit with bonds of faith and love. Traditionally, we describe this spiritual reality as the Mystical Body of Christ: a living body that breathes, reasons, and reaches out to the world in love. Openness to the church expresses itself by love for one another, dedication to serving others, and a willingness to suffer for its cause.

Jesus Christ is most powerfully encountered within this community of faith that we call the church. To love Christ is to love his church, for it is his body. As catechists, we are neither mavericks nor islands unto ourselves, but a community of people sent on a mission by the church, nourished and sheltered by the church, and empowered to bring that nourishment to others. Indeed, our physical presence as catechists is a link to the church in a very tangible way. For those whom we teach and form, we incarnate the good news as we continuously seek to reveal the person of Jesus Christ and the word of God.

"He cannot have God as his father who will not have the Church for his mother."
—Augustine of Hippo

We cannot do this authentically without being part of the church and participating in its mission.

God Is Community

You and I have been called to serve as catechists. We have a vocation. Vocations come from God through the church. We serve the mission of the church and have been authorized—entrusted with the responsibility—to proclaim the gospel message faithfully.

Living in community is not easy. It requires sacrifice. Sometimes the life of a lone ranger is appealing. It often seems easier to do things "our way." How many times have you heard someone use the expression "It's my way or the highway"? What we are asked to remember is that God's plan for each of our lives is literally the "high" way. Our true calling is to live in the image of God who is, in essence, loving community: Father, Son, and Holy Spirit.

In all that we do as catechists, our goal is to initiate and apprentice others into the life of the faith community. It is our responsibility, then, to know what the church teaches and has entrusted to us to transmit. We dedicate ourselves to learning about the church and its teachings so that we can more effectively invite others to enjoy the fruits of belonging to a community of faith.

Occasionally you might hear someone say, "Oh, we stopped going to church because there are so many hypocrites there. Yes, those people who pray on Sundays and then don't act like Christians during the week." But could you imagine the same reasoning applied to, for example, getting healthy and going to the gym? "Oh, I don't go to the gym because of all the people there who are out of shape and unhealthy. They spend their time at the gym, but it doesn't seem to make much of a difference." If we adopted this attitude in all areas of life, we would never take a risk, never develop close relationships with people, and certainly never make ourselves vulnerable.

Pope Francis often refers to the church as a "field hospital." The field hospital of the church is clearly the world in which we live, a world where people are mistreated, abused, broken, and abandoned. The church is not merely a shelter for the sinner but a hospital where restoration and healing can occur. It is a place where mercy is freely given, a sanctuary where the thirsty come to drink, and an oasis of calm in what can often seem like a jungle of chaos. We are all broken and in need of healing grace. The church is the vehicle of this healing grace, and we are blessed to participate in its life.

The Church Is a Very Large Tent

As we've mentioned already, it's not easy to share a tent with others, especially if one of them snores, one likes to stay up and read by flashlight, and another talks in his sleep! More and more, in our society, the solution is to get your own

"I am pleased to report that we have achieved our goal of doctrinal distinctiveness!"

tent—a little pup tent where you can be alone and have things exactly to your liking. We worship at the altar of individualism where no demands are placed on us save for our own preferences. Of course, privacy and solitude are valuable and even precious things. However, at our deepest core, as people made in the image of a triune God, we require community for our spiritual and mental well-being.

The Catholic Church is an immensely huge tent. Even so, there is a temptation to toss out those who don't think the same way we do and to shrink the tent so that the community will be smaller but perhaps "purer." This is not what Jesus models for us; this is not the Catholic way. For centuries, the Catholic Church has found ways to grow the tent without causing it to stretch too far or to rip. The best example of this is the wide variety of religious communities and movements that have found a home in the Church. Rather than moving apart into isolated tents, these communities and movements have created a wonderful diversity within the unity of the Church. Jesuits, Dominicans, Franciscans, Ursulines, Felicians, Carmelites, Benedictines, Claretians, Alexians, Cistercians, Marianists, Norbertines, Passionists, Redemptorists, Paulists, Vincentians, and Scalabrinians (to name just a

> **Are all apostles? Are all prophets? Are all teachers? Do all work miracles? Do all possess gifts of healing? Do all speak in tongues? Do all interpret?**
>
> —1 Corinthians 12:29–30

few)—each religious community is unique, but all belong to the one great tent called the Catholic Church.

We also have lay ecclesial movements such as Regnum Christi, Opus Dei, the Community of Sant'Egidio, the Focolare Movement, L'Arche, the Legion of Mary, and the Neocatechumenal Way—all living under the same large tent.

Finally, the Catholic Church itself, under the jurisdiction of Rome, is made up of twenty-four particular churches grouped into four rites: the Armenian, Chaldean, Byzantine, and Antiochene. Among these churches are the Latin, Alexandrian, Syriac, Coptic, Maronite, Syro-Malabar, Chaldean, Byzantine, Armenian, Ukranian, Macedonian, and Melkite churches, to name just a few. Although each rite has its own ecclesiastical, liturgical, and spiritual practices, all are entrusted to the care of the pope. In other words, they are all under the same tent. Doesn't this bring a richer understanding to the term "one, holy, catholic and apostolic"?

We would do well to remember that unity and uniformity are not the same thing. Unity means that all are invited to be sheltered under the Catholic tent precisely because each individual and community brings a unique dimension to the life of the church. Consider, for example, the parish where you serve as a catechist. Is this parish exactly like the other parishes in your town or locality? Of course not. While there is a common thread to the joys, struggles, and triumphs that each parish faces, it is also true that there is no other parish like your parish anywhere in the world. Each parish has a unique culture, traditions, and customs, all of which add to the color and composition of the church as a whole. The uniqueness of our parishes—with all of their various strengths, struggles, and challenges—makes a beautiful collage of unity within the church. As catechists, we benefit from the wide array of spiritualities that can be found in this very large tent that we call the church. Not only can we find shelter and strength in the unity within this tent, but we are also nourished by the diversity of spiritual practices that are found there.

Family Recipes

My (Joe's) daughter-in-law, Sarah, is collecting original family recipes to make into a collage. It will be a wonderful way of showing how our families have provided delicious nourishment over the years, generation after generation. It will also preserve these wonderful recipes so that future generations may enjoy them as well.

In essence, this is what we do as catechists. We're caretakers of a body of recipes—recipes that are not exclusively ours but that have been entrusted to us by the church. These "family recipes," passed down from generation to generation, are found in the Scriptures, the sacraments, the rituals, and the traditions—all the "smells and bells"—of our Catholic faith. Our role is to receive these recipes, to protect them, to share their stories, and to pass them on to the next generation. Put another way, as catechists, we are stewards of the gospel of Jesus Christ.

In order for us better to embrace our role, we catechists are called to be open to the church—not to a building or to an institution but to a living community of faith. Like a family relationship, our relationship with the church may have its ups and downs; however, it is a relationship that defines us. We strive to build up the church because it sustains us, nourishes us, and supports us throughout our life's journey. We develop this openness to the church by loving the church and its members as we do the members of our own families. We do so by showing the same respect for the leaders of the church that we are called to show our own parents. We do so by dedicating our time, talent, and treasure to the service of the church.

Food and Fellowship

In the epic trilogy *The Lord of the Rings* by the great Catholic author and scholar J. R. R. Tolkien, two hobbits, Frodo Baggins and Samwise Gamgee, set out on the journey of a lifetime. They are accompanied by a group of protectors known as "the Fellowship of the Ring." For sustenance on the perilous journey, Frodo and Sam are given a special bread called "lembas" or "waybread." In hobbit culture, these thin, crispy, light brown cakes provide strength to travelers and healing to the wounded and sick. Many readers have noted the eucharistic symbolism of lembas, since it is bread that nourishes both physically and spiritually. Without the nourishment of lembas and the protection of the fellowship, Frodo and Sam would not survive the journey. The same is true for catechists. Without the nourishment and shelter of the church, the journey would be perilous, indeed.

And we do so by patiently enduring the challenges and trials that come with being associated with Jesus Christ and his message.

Let's face it, loving our church family—like loving our first family—is not always easy. Sometimes differences of opinion cause tension and unrest. Sometimes it is hard to sit across the table from a family member who has hurt or disappointed you. But no matter what the differences between family members, the bonds that hold a family together are stronger and wider than the rifts that separate us.

One of the most profound ways that we show openness to the church is through our ongoing efforts to understand and embrace the message the church has entrusted to us. When we have difficulty understanding a particular church teaching, we don't substitute our own message in its place. Rather, we dedicate ourselves to learning more about that teaching so as to be able to proclaim it more effectively.

Your Spiritual Diet

We are what we eat. Neglecting to eat a wide array of foods will result in a nutritional imbalance within your body, and these imbalances can be quite serious. A balanced diet, on the other hand, is one that contains a variety of fresh fruits and vegetables in addition to the pantry staples that you may commonly have on hand.

All of this is true for our spiritual "diet" as well. The church offers a wide variety of foods that give us hope and sustain us on our journey of faith. As you go through the following list of common Catholic practices, or "foods," take a mental inventory of the ones that nourish you regularly and the ones that do not. Which practices would you call the "staples"? Which ones "freshen up" your spiritual diet? Which ones could you add for a more balanced diet?

- ✚ **the rosary**
- ✚ **the daily Scripture reading**
- ✚ **lectio divina**
- ✚ **adoration of the Blessed Sacrament**
- ✚ **Mass**
- ✚ **Scripture studies**
- ✚ **contemplative prayer**

- spiritual direction
- the sacrament of reconciliation
- spiritual retreat
- the Spiritual Exercises
- an examination of conscience
- novenas
- the corporal and spiritual works of mercy
- pilgrimages
- Liturgy of the Hours

Eucharist: The Ultimate Food for the Way

The Eucharist is the bread of life. We use the term *viaticum*, a Latin term meaning "for the way," to refer to a person's final earthly communion: the spiritual food for the Christian journey from earthly life to heaven. In many ways, however, all reception of the Eucharist is viaticum: this bread of life nourishes the believer on the pilgrim journey of faith and sustains us in trials, difficulties, and periods of deep joy.

As catechists, we seek and cling to hope, and we "digest" this hope throughout our lives as we are able. In her wisdom, the church knows that we cannot get through life without the hope that is nourished and sustained by the Eucharist. This food for the journey takes us across mountains, valleys, forests, hills, and plains, and one day it will take us from this earthly journey to the eternal journey we are all called to make.

A Bishop Feeds His People

In a remote area of India, a young Salesian priest named George regularly ventured into the deep recesses of the jungles and the mountains to minister to the tribes and to teach them about God. The tribes seemed to be hungry for the gospel and over time, despite great persecution, developed a strong and active faith life. The young Salesian priest was named the first bishop of the Diocese of Miao and continued his missionary efforts by educating the poorest children in India and providing medical care to whole villages ravaged by malaria and typhoid. Bishop George shared this remarkable story with me (Julianne). It is a testimony to the deep faith of the people and the determination of a bishop to bring the Eucharist to the most remote parts of the world.

Bishop George regularly visited a particularly remote tribe to celebrate Mass prior to the start of the monsoon season, when the rivers would swell so badly that the tribe would be cut off from the rest of the world for months at a time. One day, Bishop George and his group arrived on the bank of the river and were informed that conditions were too hazardous for crossing. The little dugout canoe that served as a ferry would not be able cross.

Bishop George, however, was not to be deterred. He asked one of the tribal men with a bow and arrow to shoot a rope across the river. The rope was secured around a rock on the other side so that it made a tightrope of sorts over the river. Bishop George secured his Mass kit on his head and made his way slowly and carefully through the raging water, using only the rope to guide him. Reaching the other side, he walked another four hours into the jungle so that he could celebrate Mass with the tribe. Despite the great risk to his life, he would not let the tribe down.

Today, many of us might balk at the notion of traveling even a short distance to go to Mass, let alone risk our lives to cross a raging river. And yet every day, millions of Christians around the world are willing to risk everything to encounter Jesus in the Eucharist. What are we willing to risk for Jesus?

Opening the Can of Faith for Others

Too often, backpackers bring the right foods for the journey—say, a tin of beans or a can of tuna—but forget to pack crucial utensils such as a can opener or a pot. Without these tools, preparing and eating a balanced diet is virtually impossible.

The same is true for our life of faith. Most of us can name several people who have opened up the "can of faith" for us along the way, making it possible for our spirits to be properly nourished. We can also name people who continue to bring us fresh food in the form of new and deeper insights into church teachings. Who are these people for you? How did they or do they share the food of faith with you? Take a few moments to give thanks for them and their generosity.

Before he became our Holy Father, Pope Francis—Cardinal Jorge Mario Bergoglio—explained that disciples of Christ must not approach believing as a private act since we are all sons or daughters of the church.

A Prayer for Those Who Have Shared Their Faith

Heavenly Father, I give thanks for those who share their Catholic faith with me generously and lovingly. Just as Jesus fed the multitudes with five loaves and two fish, may I be able to share most generously the faith that you have given me in love. Help me be a grateful steward of this faith, freely sharing my time, talent, and treasure with others. I ask this through the Holy Name of Jesus. Amen.

While it is true that there is a private dimension to our faith, faith first comes to us through others. Many of us first learned what to believe and how to practice our faith from family members, friends, and early teachers. Catechists are key figures in this process. As a catechist, you are the "can opener" of faith for those you teach—the means by which the spiritual food of the church is made accessible. You also provide the fork and spoon with which God's people are fed.

The expression "How do you eat an elephant? One bite at a time!" is a good reminder for us as we break open church teachings and help people apply those teachings to their lives. Like health care workers, we catechists know that sometimes you have to spoon-feed people until they are ready to feed themselves. When simple foods are swallowed and digested with ease, it may be time to try more complex tastes and textures. And when certain foods are rejected, we are not deterred. Even though a little "spit-up" may be discouraging and unpleasant, we remain patient and determined to fulfill our task of feeding God's people. As catechists, we stay attentive to the signs of readiness for more or less "food," for difficult concepts, for deeper understanding, and for the opportunity to experience the mystery of the church in ever deeper and more profound ways.

> I fed you with milk, not solid food, for you were not ready for solid food. Even now you are still not ready.
>
> —1 Corinthians 3:2

A Body in Motion

Let's revisit our little nursery rhyme one more time:

> Here is the church.
> Here is the steeple.
> Open the doors and see all the people.
> Close the doors and let them pray.
> Open the doors and they've all gone away.

The church as the body of Christ is a body in motion. It is an active, living and breathing family of those who come together and are nourished and restored to health. Note that the movement in this nursery rhyme is from a people "being" to a people "doing." Before undertaking any work of the church, it is essential that we have a firm commitment to the church and are grounded in prayer. Without them, our efforts will not be as effective or as wide-reaching.

Open the Doors and They've All Gone Away

This is the great beauty and treasure of the church. When its doors are opened, we leave renewed to take and share what we have received with others. Nourished and sheltered under the big tent of Catholicism, the people of God are out in the world right this minute. They are feeding the hungry, taking care of the sick, educating children, and forming adults in faith. Now that is the ultimate backpacking adventure!

Questions for Reflection

> Think of a family heirloom you have been entrusted with. What story is connected with this heirloom? How do you guard and protect it? How and to whom do you intend to pass it on?
> Who are the people who have entrusted the gospel message to you? (They may be family, friends, pastors, teachers, catechists, professors, and so on.) Through whom did you receive your calling to serve as a catechist? How did this calling come about?
> Describe your sense of belonging when it comes to the church. Is your sense of belonging strong or could it use some strengthening?
> What challenges and frustrations do you experience in family life? What joys do you experience? In your relationship with the church, what challenges, frustrations, and joys do you experience?

> What church teaching do you have difficulty understanding? What can you do to deepen your understanding of this and other church teachings? What is a teaching that you have come to understand better recently?
> What sacrifices do you face as a catechist? How do you feel about these sacrifices and challenges? Why do you endure them?
> What do you or can you do to deepen your commitment to the church?
> Whom do you know who exhibits a great commitment to the church? How can you emulate him or her?
> How does your commitment to the church affect you in your role as a catechist?
> How can you help those you teach to be more open to the church?
> What's your favorite family recipe? What is the story behind it? How has this recipe been passed through your family? What is your plan for passing it along?
> Why do you love the church? What moments in your life have confirmed and reconfirmed this love?
> If you had to describe your relationship with the church in one word, what would it be? Why?
> Do you feel a sense of responsibility to and for the church? How does this manifest itself in your life?

For Further Reflection

"I prefer a Church which is bruised, hurting and dirty because it has been out on the streets, rather than a Church which is unhealthy from being confined and from clinging to its own security. I do not want a Church concerned with being at the centre and which then ends by being caught up in a web of obsessions and procedures. If something should rightly disturb us and trouble our consciences, it is the fact that so many of our brothers and sisters are living without the strength, light and consolation born of friendship with Jesus Christ, without a community of faith to support them, without meaning and a goal in life."

—Pope Francis, *Evangelii Gaudium*

Spiritual Exercises

The following spiritual exercises are designed to deepen your commitment to the church and to ensure that the nourishment of the church is an essential element in your catechist's backpack. Consider sharing the fruits of your exercises with a friend or a fellow catechist.

> Think about your oldest church-related possession. Is it your First Communion prayer book and rosary? Is it a scapular? Is it your baptismal gown? Locate this special heirloom and place it in the space where you pray for the coming week as a reminder of your relationship with the church. Read and reflect on John 17, Jesus' prayer for the church.

> In the coming week, pray each day for a different person who was instrumental in passing on the Catholic faith to you. Reflect on how these people did so and how you can emulate them in your vocation as a catechist. Pray in a special way for the leaders of the church: the pope, the bishops, the clergy, and the lay ecclesial ministers who are responsible for transmitting the faith.

> In the coming week, spend some time reflecting on your own understanding of the four "pillars" of the Catechism of the Catholic Church: the creed, the sacraments, morality, and prayer. Reflect on one pillar a day over the next four days. Journal about your own understanding of each pillar.

> Creed: What beliefs are at the core of your Catholic faith?
> Sacraments: How have you encountered or do you encounter Jesus in the sacraments?
> Morality: What is your understanding of Catholic morality?
> Prayer: Why and how do you pray?

> Which of these areas most needs your attention as you deepen your understanding of the Catholic faith? Commit to an opportunity to attend to it this year.

> Reflect on the following quote from the *Guide for Catechists*: "Through religious instruction, preparation for the sacraments, animation of prayer and other works of charity, [catechists] help the baptized to grow in the fervor of the Christian life. . . . Often, they are called to witness to their faith by harsh trials and painful privations. The history of evangelization past and present attests to their constancy even to the giving of life itself. Catechists are truly the pride of the missionary Church!" Do you believe that you are an irreplaceable part of the

missionary outreach of the church? How do you strive to communicate this understanding to your friends, your family, and your students? Have you suffered harsh trials in your catechetical journey? What or who carried you through these times?

> Take out your class roster and go through the names on your list. Ponder in your heart the students whom you instruct in the faith. Make a note of those students who are ready for more complicated flavors and foods; make a note of those students who are not yet ready to explore more adventurous food; and, finally, make a note of those students who might need even milder or simpler food for now. Think about the kinds of foods you might introduce in your class and in what order. Give thanks to God for all these students. Offer up a prayer of gratitude.

What Catechists Are Saying about Commitment to the Church

❝Church to me today is the people I worship with . . . and the community that comes together. A deacon told us once that if what you hear in these four walls stays in these four walls, then we are not being church. What we hear in these four walls has to be taken out and shared with all of the people outside. That is church. That is how I feel about my parish. It is my home.

—Karen

The spiritual union with church family members is the same as it is with nuclear family members: the shared pain and sufferings with others and the joy of being able to come together with others to make a difference through prayer; the understanding of the interconnectedness of us all to each other. The revealing of the interconnectedness with God already going on in our lives and how being open to his guidance in prayer can bring us the happiness we seek.

—Val

I grew up in my parish, and my church community is like a second family to me. I want to share something that I saved from our parish bulletin: "This is my parish. It is composed of people like me. We will make it what it is. It will be friendly, if I am. Its pews will be filled, if I help to fill them. It will make generous gifts to many causes, if I am a generous giver. It will bring other people to its worship and fellowship, if I bring them. It will be a church of loyalty and love, of fearlessness and faith, and a church with a noble spirit, if I, who make it what it is, am filled with these qualities. Therefore, with the

help of God, I shall dedicate myself to the task of being all things that I want my church to be."
—Bernie

The Church is my family. I receive strength, encouragement, and love. I am learning more about the power of the Eucharist through Mass and Holy Hour. Now, I need to trust in the healing graces of the nightly examination of conscience and reconciliation. I want to pass all this on to the students whom he has entrusted to me for so short a time.
—Dorothy

My sense of belonging goes back to about fifteen years ago when I was working in Washington, D.C., and went to a different church every Sunday, including the [Episcopal] National Cathedral. The only churches I felt comfortable in were St. Matthew's Cathedral and the Basilica of the Immaculate Conception. I realized I was meant to be a Catholic.
—Steve

My sense of belonging within the church actually overwhelms me. I can think of numerous times within the past couple of years when I've had questions, and regardless of who answered them, whether the pastor or DRE or someone at the diocese, I was SO warmly received with an answer. I've often said, "I felt like they were waiting for me to call them." I try to share with others (whether friends that have fallen away from the Church or a brother that may be skeptical of the help anyone in the parish could give him) that if you don't reach out, you will never know.
—Greg

The church has always been a stabilizing influence in my life, a place of comfort and refuge. When I was twelve years old, my parents divorced, and the huge void that opened in my heart through that experience still takes my breath away today. My home life was never the same. During the pain of that experience, however, it was the people in my church family that held me together and helped me through the worst of times. I didn't realize until I went to college and didn't have a parish home how much being a part of a parish meant to me. Since coming back to the faith as an adult, I find that the church, which has always loved and prayed for me, is my true home. 〞
—Allen

Chapter 3

Openness to the World: A Topographical Map

Catechists, therefore, will be open and attentive to the needs of the world, knowing that they are called to work in and for the world, without however belonging completely to it. This means that they must be thoroughly involved in the life of the society about them, without pulling back from fear of difficulties or withdrawing through love of tranquility. But they must keep a supernatural outlook on life and trust in the efficacy of God's word, which does not return to Him without "succeeding in what it was sent to do" (Isaiah 55:11).   *—Guide for Catechists*, no. 7

Becoming Familiar with the Terrain

When backpacking in an unfamiliar location, it's important to have some navigational assistance—a map or a compass—and some basic information about the wildlife and plant life in the area. These resources usually prove helpful and sometimes prove life-saving.

Similarly, on the catechist's journey, it is crucial that we familiarize ourselves with the "terrain" of this world. The Holy Spirit was poured forth so that we would proclaim the gospel to all nations. The Holy Spirit serves as our map, our compass, and ultimately our "GPSS"—our global positioning spiritual system. Without the Holy Spirit, we would wander aimlessly.

> On the catechist's journey, it is crucial that we familiarize ourselves with the "terrain" of this world.

Catechists are called to be uniquely in touch with the field in which the seeds of the gospel are to be sown: the world. We are called, however, not simply to immerse ourselves in the world but to survey it thoroughly, engage, and challenge it so that it may be transformed in and through Christ.

The Times, They Are A'Changin'

So, let me ask you a question: do you tweet?

Years ago, if someone asked you to tweet, you might consider chirping like a bird. Of course, nowadays, to tweet means to send a short message on the social-networking site Twitter. For many of us, however, it's like speaking a new language. Not that long ago, if someone said he had Googled your spouse, you might've punched him in the mouth. Commonly used words that have been added to the Oxford English Dictionary in recent years include *bling, chillax, Twitterati, upcycle,* and *hacking*. Do you know the meanings of these words? Keeping up with the times is hard work and the times—well, they are a'changin'.

But what does all this have to do with being a catechist?

In *Gaudium et Spes* from the Second Vatican Council, we read the following: "The Church has always had the duty of scrutinizing the signs of the times and of interpreting them in the light of the Gospel." In order to scrutinize the signs of the times, however, we catechists must first recognize and be familiar with them. This doesn't mean that we should allow "the world"— society, politics, culture—to set the agenda for catechesis. But it does mean that we are to be in touch with this ever-changing world, looking for entry points into the lives of those we teach. St. Ignatius of Loyola called this process entering through their door, but leaving through your own. Our task is to identify these "doorways" and introduce through them the light of Christ, trusting it to illuminate what is good and to expose what needs to be transformed.

> "The Church has always had the duty of scrutinizing the signs of the times and of interpreting them in the light of the Gospel."
>
> —*GAUDIUM ET SPES*, NO. 4

So what does this mean in terms of our spirituality? It means that we can and must pray for the needs of the world. God wants the entire world to be saved. The Good News is for all people—not just those who are close to us, sound like us, look like us, and think like us. It is not just for those who attend Mass on Sunday but also for those who live on the margins and outskirts of society. The Good News is "good" for a reason! The Good News has something to offer each person as a child of God. The spirituality of the catechist calls us to expand our circle of concern to pray for the needs of all people.

To be open to the world means that we are called to both action and contemplation, recognizing that our own efforts will not transform society but that the grace of God encountered

"Rachel has a gift for working with kids."

in prayer will work through us to bring about this transformation. This both/and dynamic is expressed most beautifully in the persons of John, the Beloved Disciple, and Peter, the Rock. Peter was a man of action—hotheaded, passionate, and rash. "Engage brain before opening mouth" would have been a helpful mantra for him! John, on the other hand, is depicted as contemplative and reflective; he was the one who leaned against Jesus and listened to his heartbeat during the Last Supper. Both men were chosen by Jesus, both were loved, both were valued. Both action and contemplation have equal value in the church.

To be open to the world is to open our minds and hearts to those who do not share or appreciate gospel values. As teachers, the challenge comes in loving the obstinate participant in our class, knowing that Jesus came to gather all to himself—especially those who are in need of his healing embrace.

In the Scripture episode known as the Great Commission, Jesus sends his own disciples to "Go . . . and make disciples of all nations" (Matthew 28:16–20). Notice that Jesus says *all* nations. He does not tell his followers to withdraw from the world, but rather to go headlong into it. In John's Gospel, Jesus prays to his heavenly Father, "I am not asking you to take them out of the world, but I ask you to protect them from the evil one . . . As you have sent me into the world, so I have sent them into the world" (John 17:15, 18). So look out, world—here come the catechists!

Finding God in All Things

Sheep, fishing nets, pearls, coins, buried treasures, wine, wineskins, yeast, mustard seeds, fig trees, vineyards, tenants, and banquets: these are just a few of the images Jesus used when he taught. These images were familiar to Jesus' audience, and so he used them to capture the imagination of the crowds. By speaking to their everyday experiences, he helped them find God in all things.

We catechists are called to do the same. The everyday experiences of the young people we teach may involve such phenomena as the Cloud, Pinterest, spyware, Instagram, Facebook, YouTube, gigabytes, mashups, webinars, bandwidth, Bluetooth, Bitcoin, Google, GPS, MP3s, and so on. No doubt these terms sound like a foreign language to some of us. But if we hope to be open to the world as Jesus was, this is a language we'll have to learn.

He *Had* to Go Through Samaria?

From his humble beginnings onward, Jesus showed openness to the world. The Incarnation itself is an example of the profound openness of God to the world. God did not disdain the ordinariness of this world, but instead "so loved the world that he gave his only Son, so that everyone who believes in him may not perish but may have eternal life" (John 3:16).

Jesus was sinless, and yet he entered the Jordan River to be baptized with sinners. He did not need forgiveness, but still he chose to stand shoulder to shoulder with sinners. He even called one of his closest friends and followers, Matthew, from a profession despised by the people—that of tax collector. Tax collectors were viewed as greedy, corrupt, and selfish. They often colluded with the Roman authorities for profit and so were both hated and feared by the average person. And yet, because of Jesus' openness

A middle-aged catechist wanted to appear "with it" to her junior high class, so she asked one of her students what type of computer he had. The boy responded, "I have a computer with Intel Core i7 processor at 3.3 GHz, Windows 7, 64 bit, 8gb RAM and a Nvidia gtx 560 graphics card. What kind do you have?" After a long pause, the embarrassed catechist responded, "A pink one."

Praying Hands

The interlacing of heaven and earth, spirit and matter, God and humanity is expressed most beautifully in the postures that we adopt in prayer. Holding our hands together reflects the human and the divine nature coming together in the Incarnation. Each time we clasp our hands and intertwine our fingers, our fingers point up to the heavens, just as our prayers do. That song we teach our children—"He's got the whole world in his hands"—is true. He's got the whole world in his hands; he's got the whole world in his hands. Thank God for that!

to him, Matthew's life was radically transformed. He traded in comfort and wealth for poverty and simplicity. He traded in a life of domination for one of service. He became a collector of souls for Christ rather than a collector of money for the empire.

Jesus' openness to the world is also evidenced in his traveling itinerary between Judea and Galilee. In Jesus' time, it was customary for Jews who were traveling this route to avoid passing through Samaria. Jesus, however, did no such thing. In fact, according to the Gospel of John, Jesus "had to pass through Samaria" (John 4:4). He *had* to? This tiny helping verb tells us something important. It tells us that Jesus went voluntarily into foreign territory because it was part of his mission.

Now *that's* openness to the world. Jesus himself did not flee from the world. Rather, he plunged headlong into the ordinariness of life to reveal the extraordinary presence of God there. Jesus did not tell his followers to run and hide or to separate from society. Rather, he said to them, "Go!"

That same commission is meant for us. As catechists, we are sent forth into the world. Each time we teach, we are called to enter into the world of those we teach. We may not fully understand "their world." We may not approve of everything that is happening in "their world." However, we must resist thinking that somehow God is more present in "our world." Our task is to enter into their

> But he had to go through Samaria.
> —John 4:4

Finding God in the Ordinary

At St. Nicholas Cathedral in Galway, Ireland, there is an extraordinary stained-glass window depicting the Holy Family. It is extraordinary in its ordinariness. Jesus is depicted as a little red-haired boy (it's an Irish Jesus after all!) clad in the britches customary for young boys in times past. In his hands is a cup of tea that he is taking to his foster father, Joseph, who is in the background planing a piece of wood. Joseph's head is down, and he is focused on his work. Seated in the corner is the Blessed Mother. What is Mary doing? She is sitting barefoot by the fire, knitting! In contrast to the traditional depictions of the Holy Family, the family in this window is simple, accessible, and warm. Each time I look at it, I am reminded of my own family. I remember how we become holy in and through the ordinary moments of our lives—through our work, our hobbies, and in spending time with those we love.   —Julianne

world and to help them uncover and recognize the God who is already there.

Sprechen Sie Deutsch?

Traveling to a foreign country where English is not the primary language can be quite a challenge. Letting go of one's own language and seeking to comprehend another is both difficult and transformative. When one is able to do so, new experiences become possible.

Quite often, those we teach "speak a different language." In some cases, this is literally true. In most cases, it is metaphorically true. Being open to the world means learning to speak the language of those we teach. In our multicultural world, there are a variety of languages that we as catechists must be familiar with. This doesn't necessarily mean learning Spanish, Vietnamese, or Polish. Rather, it means learning to speak the language of so-called millennials, of the Baby Boomers, of the elderly, of preschool children, of junior high students, of young parents, of those in mid-life, and of those in primary and intermediate grades. It also means learning to speak the language of inner-city kids as well as those from rural environments, of those who are well-to-do and those who are struggling to make ends meet, of women and men, of Democrats and Republicans, of those who are married and those who aren't, and of those who are gay and those who are straight. In doing so, we become capable of doing what St. Ignatius of Loyola taught his catechists to do: entering through their door, but leaving through their own.

Let's pray for ourselves and for one another that we may have a true openness to the world—not disdaining it, but entering into it as Jesus did. Only in this way can we help others recognize God in their midst.

St. Patrick's Openness to the World

When I (Julianne) was a child, I loved to do pencil rubbings of the ornate patterns on Celtic crosses. The Celtic cross is found throughout the world in art and jewelry and is often referenced in literature, music, and poetry. Each Celtic cross is unique, but its distinguishing feature is an orb or halo that encircles the cross-section of the two beams. This feature has significance. When he came to Ireland, St. Patrick encountered a pagan people who worshiped the sun. In order to make the veneration of the cross seem more natural to the people, St. Patrick encircled it. With this simple addition, he created a cross that evoked both the sun that lights the sky and the Son who is the light of the world. His openness to the language of the people not only transformed Ireland, but gave Christians all over the world a clear and lasting symbol of Christ's light.

Turn on Your Cell Phones!

It is customary in catechetical and worship settings to remind people to turn off or silence their cell phones. Many catechists today, however, are changing tack. Instead of instructing participants to turn off their phones, they ask them to put their phones to work. Participants can use their phones to access social media and "check in" from their parish to let others know where they are and what they're doing. Likewise, they might use their phones to look up information on the Internet as part of a lesson or activity. Some pastors are even inviting worshipers to tweet a line from the Gospel or the homily that speaks to their heart. The bottom line is, being open to the world means exploring how to use the things of this world to help those you teach find and share God.

The orb or halo of the Celtic cross often depicts scenes from nature interwoven with scenes from Scripture. This, too, is a powerful reminder that God reveals himself both in the Word *and* in the world. It reminds us that the world itself is a living sacrament, the gift of a loving God to his beloved children. When we begin to see the world as revelation and sacrament, we can't help but open ourselves to it. This profound sense of openness to the world in turn enables us as catechists to help others find God in their daily living.

Smelling Like the Sheep We Shepherd

Pope Francis is known for the many clever and powerful insights offered in his audiences, homilies, and written works. One of his most famous lines was delivered to the world's priests at the Chrism Mass on Holy Thursday, 2013. "A priest who seldom goes out of himself," the pope said, "misses out on the best of our people, on what can stir the depths of his priestly heart. . . . This is precisely the reason why some priests grow dissatisfied, lose heart and become in a sense collectors of antiquities or novelties—instead of being shepherds living with 'the smell of the sheep.' This is what I am asking you—be shepherds with the smell of sheep." One priest, when told of the Holy Father's words, remarked, "Well, some of the sheep smell pretty bad." That's precisely the point. Ministry, catechesis in particular, does not take place in a sterile environment. We ourselves may not be as fragrant as we think!

As catechists, we need to be close to our sheep, not distant. This doesn't mean that we should become absorbed into their world or that we need to try to identify with them. It means that we are to be in touch with their reality so that we can speak to it, affirm that which is good and holy, and address in a spirit of charity that which is not.

The truth is that sometimes our relationships with others and with God can be messy. And yet, it is precisely within that messiness that God can often be encountered. In order to emphasize this point, one bishop developed the habit of applying so much oil to confirmation candidates that he created a mess on their foreheads. When asked why he was being so

> "Would you like to honor the body of Christ you receive in the Eucharist? Do not despise the poor when you see him clothed in rags."
> —St. John Chrysostom

generous in his application of the holy oil, the bishop responded, "I do this because the sacraments place us at the intersection of the deepest moments of people's lives—death, illness, marriage, baptism, life. I lavish the oil on the candidates so that they can feel just how effuse and potent God's love is for them and how it can penetrate and loosen the bonds of our hearts. I do so because God's love is not stingy and neither is my application!"

Watch Out for Those Potholes!

We, the authors, live in Chicago and Green Bay—cities well known for their brutal winters. When the snow melts every spring, we encounter the reality of potholes in our streets. Unlike the bumps and ditches in construction zones, potholes are not marked by warning signs. As a result, they often take a toll on our wheel alignment. In a similar way, our journey as catechists is full of unmarked potholes. While it does bring wonderful rewards ("out of this world" rewards, some would say), there are days when the road feels more like an obstacle course. On these days, we find ourselves in need of spiritual alignment.

In every backpacker's journey, there comes a time when the terrain gets steadily more difficult or veers into unexpected or hazardous territory. At times like this, a careful review of a map or navigational system can help. It can calm us down and arm us with the knowledge we need to avoid obstacles that may otherwise push us to our physical, mental, and spiritual limits. Taking a break can be the catalyst we need to refuel and reorient ourselves before picking up the trail again. During these moments, we would also do well to remember that Jesus himself tells us that he has conquered the world and we don't have to do it all on our own! Whew!

Are We There Yet?

If you've ever gone on a road trip with children, you've probably heard this question (or maybe even asked it yourself). It is a natural question, one appropriate not only to road trips but to the faith journey, too—especially when we encounter life's potholes or when our path veers off course.

"I have said this to you, so that in me you may have peace. In the world you face persecution. But, take courage; I have conquered the world."

—John 16:33

A wise friend once reminded me (Julianne) that "the straight and narrow path is the one that doesn't seem to have a traffic problem." Living in a busy world, it is easy for us to focus either on where we've been or on where we're going and forget to enjoy the journey itself. Worrying about the past or the future isn't a fruitful spiritual endeavor, and yet sometimes we cannot help but fall into worry or doubt. St. Augustine taught that we need to entrust the past to God's mercy, the present to the love of God, and the future to the providence of God. Wise words, indeed.

When we find ourselves haunted by the past or anxious about the future, it is good to hit pause, to reset our "GPSS"—our global positioning spiritual system—and to spend some time reflecting on the Lord's presence on our journey. This can be done in private prayer or with a trusted friend or spiritual mentor. Doing so can help us recall that, although we are not there yet, we are right where God wants us to be— in the world. It is in this world, and only in this world, that we can discover God and help others do the same.

Questions for Reflection

> What are some recent advances in society or technology that have made your head spin?
> What would you include in a time capsule for this day and age, in the place where you live? Why?
> What disturbing trends do you see in society today? What encouraging trends do you see?
> How would you describe the "doorway" into the lives of those you teach? In other words, what are they most fascinated with, worried about, or skilled at? What simple steps could you take to walk through that door?
> What are some strategies you have used to speak your students' language? What are some strategies you could use?
> What is the greatest need of those you teach?
> Who are those who need a little extra time, attention, and prayer among those you teach or have taught? How can you pray for them?
> Who is someone you know who is open to the world but does not "belong" to it? Who was a teacher you had who was open to the world? How can you emulate him or her?
> How can being open to the world make you a more effective catechist?

> What can and will you do on your faith journey to be more open to the world?
> In what ways do you feel that you have conformed to values that are not consistent with the gospel? How might you become more conscious of this and how might you change this?
> In what ways do you feel that God has worked through you to transform your own "world" and the "world" of those you teach?
> Who in your life keeps you in touch with the Holy Spirit—your "GPSS," or global positioning spiritual system? Why do you think it is important to have a spiritual mentor or friend on the journey?
> What are the best ways you know to hit the pause or reset button?

For Further Reflection

Read the preface and introductory statement of *Gaudium et Spes*, from the Second Vatican Council, which urges us to be open to the world.

Spiritual Exercises

The following spiritual exercises are designed to deepen your openness to the world. Feel free to share the fruits of your exercises with another catechist or a group of catechists.

> Spend this week praying with the daily news (whether you receive it through the TV, newspaper, Internet, or social media). Scan the news to observe what is going on, and then take these events and happenings to prayer. Ask God to help you recognize the needs of others in the world. Ask for the grace to see how you can make connections between the events of today's world and the events of the gospel in your catechesis.
> Spend some of your prayer time this week trying to get into the "shoes" of those you teach. What are they concerned about? What worries do they have? What joys are they experiencing? What events are occurring in their lives? What needs and desires do they have? Bring all these to prayer, asking God to help you know the minds and hearts of those you teach and to make you sensitive to their needs.
> The earliest followers of Christ prayed for the courage to venture into new territories to bring the word of God to others. Pray this week for the courage to enter into a new "territory." This new territory might be a form of technology that your learners are familiar with, a new social

medium, a new genre of music or art, or even a new way of saying "hello." Then take steps to help your prayer come true.

> Reflect on the following prayer from St. Patrick. What images in the prayer speak to you? What phrase or word holds particular meaning for you? Consider the sentence "the glorious sun's life giving ray." Read it again as follows: "the glorious Son's life giving rays." Now, reflect on the life-giving rays of Christ in your life. What other metaphors do you notice in the prayer?

> *I bind unto myself today*
> *The virtues of the starlit heaven,*
> *The glorious sun's life giving ray,*
> *The whiteness of the moon at even,*
> *The flashing of the lightning free,*
> *The whirling wind's tempestuous shocks,*
> *The stable earth, the deep salt sea,*
> *Around the old eternal rocks.*
> *I bind unto myself today*
> *The power of God to hold and lead,*
> *His eye to watch, his might to stay,*
> *His ear to hearken to my need,*
> *The wisdom of my god to teach,*
> *His hand to guide, his shield to ward,*
> *The Word of God to give me speech,*
> *His heavenly host to be my guard.*
> *Amen.*

—*The* Lorica *of St. Patrick*

> Opening ourselves to the world can start right where we live. When Pope Francis speaks of "going to the margins," he wants us to broaden our understanding of where the margins are and who might live in them. Consider your neighborhood. Consider those in your family. Consider those with whom you live and work who have been bruised, hurt, and wounded. How can your family or neighborhood become a place where those on the margins feel included?

> For centuries, stained-glass windows allowed those who were illiterate to "read" the Christian story. Consider the stained-glass windows in your parish church or in another church in your community. Find out the history behind the windows, who made them, and why they chose particular symbols. Consider taking your students to see and learn

about the windows. If you teach younger children, convert images of the windows into coloring pages so that they, too, can learn about the local church and the universal church in a simple and creative way.

What Catechists Are Saying about Openness to the World

❝"Our task is to enter into their world and to help them uncover and recognize the God who is already there" . . . I love this. Great job description for "catechist." Working with teens, this is even more of a challenge. I find that many times my time and energy is spent in programming according to what I perceive as young people's needs, or their parents' needs, or the parish's needs. . . . Making the starting point young people and their needs, their world, their hurts, their concerns is so important. Lord, help me to jump in and swim with the young people. Be my swimmies, help me to go the distance, help me brave the cold water sometimes. *—Linda*

I used to teach computer technology and the religion classes would come to me to make PowerPoints such as scriptural rosaries, Stations of the Cross, religious web sites, and so forth. I made a really good one of the Stations using the Passion of the Christ which was really popular a few years ago. I regularly use my iPod and my cell phone, both of which can play MP3 files as spiritual resources. I look at Creighton's *Daily Meditations* and listen to *Pray as You Go*. I obviously look at web sites such as *Catechist's Journey*. *—Steve*

I am a big believer that the good can overwhelm the bad. For example, we (as a society) spend so much time worrying about our kids online and the predators or porn or violence that are out there. These are real threats to our kids, of course. But if we can promote the good stuff and show our kids how much "cool" stuff there is online related to the faith, I think we can overwhelm the bad stuff. *—Greg*

Maybe openness to the world doesn't mean I have to have a PC in class. For me, maybe it means I'm a little more up on the teen scene with regard to issues . . . and am not afraid to bring them up in class. I did some "moral dilemma" exercises last year and I know I could go a lot deeper on some of those topics. I guess it's not all about technology but, rather, focusing on what these twelve to fourteen year olds face today. More thought needed on that one but just sharing where I'm at right now. *—Jean*

At the beginning of the school year, I have my second graders fill out a simple questionnaire—name, age, and such—but then we get to the heart of it and ask, What's your favorite movie, food, TV show . . . If God were here right now what would you ask him (always a great one) . . . What did you learn last year in CCD and what did you like to do while in class (always an eye-opener). This is how I begin to learn about the kids and their interests, sometimes about their home life, and how I will begin to engage with the class based on some of the answers I receive. Sometimes it takes a while for the kids to open up about their individual needs, but the key to every new class is to listen carefully each week. The needs do come to light and I usually try to focus as they do.   —Anne

I worked at a secular school where overt displays of faith such as religious art were discouraged. I often shared with my friend just how difficult it was to work in an environment devoid of the symbolism of our faith, where I felt uncomfortable hanging an image of the Last Supper in my office, for example. Out of the blue, my friend sent me a package to "keep the faith"—a little bottle of mustard seeds that one could use in cooking. This little bottle of seeds was placed prominently on my desk as a reminder to me that every moment of my workday was an opportunity to conduct myself as a person of faith in small and sometimes not so small ways.   —Veronica

I cannot tell you how many times I have heard from other parents that I shouldn't allow my children to read books like Harry Potter! Knowing my children well and reading the books with them (at an age-appropriate time) gave me a window into what characteristics, ideas, and images appealed to them. I think reading the books also made me a better catechist because I was able to connect with the students in my classes better and help them view the Harry Potter themes of self-sacrifice, trust, hope, and death through the lens of our Catholic faith. 🙷🙷   —Michael

Chapter 4

Consistency and Authenticity: The Right Clothing and Footwear

> Before *doing* the catechesis one must first of all *be* a catechist. The *truth* of their lives confirms their message. It would be sad if they did not *"practice what they preached"* and spoke about a God of whom they had theoretical knowledge but with whom they had no contact.
>
> —*Guide for Catechists*, no. 8

Gear That's Made for the Job

Few things can ruin a backpacking adventure like inadequate clothing and footwear. In order to maintain a good pace and withstand the elements, a backpacker needs clothing and shoes that are made for hiking.

As catechists, we also need "clothing" made for the job and its ever-changing terrain. Fortunately, we received just the right clothing when, in baptism, we "put on Christ." Christ is not a costume we can put on and take off as we please. When we "put on Christ," we enter into relationship with him. To wear Christ is to be intimate with him; to wear Christ as a catechist is to show and share this intimacy with our students.

Authenticity

In a *Forbes* article titled "What Is Authentic Leadership?" author, speaker, and entrepreneur Kevin Kruse expresses dismay that so many leaders act one way at work and another way outside of work—and then are surprised when their employees don't trust them or like them. What Kruse is getting at is this: authenticity is a key concept in leadership and in the marketing world.

Think, for example, about the foods you choose to cook with and to eat. Chances are you prefer foods labeled "natural" or "made from natural

What Consumers Really Want

In their book *Authenticity: What Consumers Really Want*, authors James H. Gilmore and B. Joseph Pine II assert that consumers seek to purchase authentic products from genuine people rather than settling for something that's fake from someone that's phony. They also point out that consumers seek not only goods and services, but also experiences that personally engage them.

This is true for catechists, too. The primary job of a catechist is to provide an experience of encountering Christ. And that experience must be authentic—genuine—and not phony.

ingredients" rather than those labeled "made with artificial ingredients and preservatives." You may recall the ingredients and brands the cook in your house used in certain dishes when you were growing up. Did your mother insist on a particular kind of shortening in her pie crusts? Did your dad insist on a certain pancake mix? If so, it was because they believed those products were authentic—the real thing! Now think of your own preferences or those of your kids. Do you know someone who won't try any other brand of peanut butter than the one they've always used? Of course you do!

Let's face it, we tend to be creatures of habit, especially when it comes to our preferences. And most of us prefer products we consider authentic over those we consider counterfeit. Authenticity and brand loyalty often drive consumer preferences for everything from cars to pasta sauce to soda. (Remember Coca-Cola's long-time slogan, "It's the real thing"?)

To help those we teach encounter Christ, we, too, must be "the real thing." We would be wise to take a lesson from marketing, which tells us that authenticity is what results when there is a harmony between what one is and what one does—and, we would add,

> **Authenticity is what results when there is a harmony between what one is and what one does.**

what one says. Today's world is a "world of mouth," where what we say and post online and chat about often holds tremendous power for those around us. Take social media, for example. A large percentage of people's "friends" or "followers" choose to "creep," or monitor their friends' posts or statuses without interacting with them. They make mental notes of our likes, preferences, beliefs, and inclinations and draw conclusions about the kind of people we are. It should come as no surprise, then, to know that our students are studying us, too, and monitoring us for authenticity. We must strive to be sure that there is no gap between who we are as human beings and what we do and say as catechists. When there is harmony between our "real selves" and our "catechist selves," we telegraph authenticity or integrity—a consistency between what we say, how we act, and how we live.

"We're here to see if you practice what you preach."

Under the Microscope

This point bears emphasizing: those we teach are watching us closely for signs of authenticity and consistency. We are very much "under the microscope." We need to be mindful that even the kind of clothing or jewelry we wear speaks its own language to the students. We need to ask ourselves if our clothing is distracting, "loud," or immodest, or if it matches what we believe in and who we are. How might this be perceived by our students?

In particular, our students are seeking consistency between:

➕ our words in class and our actions outside of class. Do we practice what we preach? If a student turned up at your home, would he or she know it was a Christian home? Would he or she know it was a Catholic home? How?

➕ our words and our body language. Do we look as though we are proclaiming Good News? Do our faces show the joy of Christ? What attitude do we project when we speak about church teachings we find personally difficult? Would a student be able to perceive disdain or disregard? How can we project respect and humility instead?

➕ the concepts we teach and our manner of interacting with students. Do we preach love, patience, and forgiveness, and then speak or act harshly? How do we handle disciplinary issues in the classroom? How do we handle the pressure of getting a lesson finished on time? Do students see you as harried, haphazard, and critical, or fair, deliberate, and prepared?

Those we teach will experience the gospel as authentic if they experience *us* as authentic. This is what the church has in mind when it says, "No methodology, no matter how well tested, can dispense with the person of the cate-chist in every phase of the catechetical process."

Faith formation might involve glossy textbooks, glitzy videos, rousing music, and dizzying Internet connections, but none of it will mean anything unless the person "on the ground," interacting with the learners, is an authentic disciple of Jesus Christ. The fact of the matter is that while programs and resources can be a springboard for deepening faith, disciples are formed by disciples.

> **No methodology, no matter how well tested, can dispense with the person of the catechist in every phase of the catechetical process.**
> —*General Directory for Catechesis*, no. 156

It's the Pits!

There was a fable of sorts floating around on the Internet a while back. There were many different versions of the story, but it went mostly like this:

> A man fell into a pit and could not get himself out.
>
> A subjective person said, "I feel really bad for you down there."
>
> An objective person said, "How could someone possibly fall down there?"
>
> A Pharisee said, "Only bad people would fall into such a pit."
>
> A news reporter wanted an exclusive story on the pit—the *who, what, where*, and *why*.
>
> A mathematician calculated how he fell into the pit.
>
> The IRS agent asked if he was paying taxes on the pit.
>
> A self-pitying person said, "You haven't seen anything until you have seen my pit."
>
> An optimist said, "Things could get worse."
>
> A pessimist said, "Things will get worse."
>
> A realist said, "Yep, that's quite a pit you are in there."
>
> But Jesus, seeing the man, took him by the hand, and lifted him up out of the pit.

The pit, in a sense, represents the patterns of sin we all fall into at some point in our lives. At these times, we are unable to see our way out of the pit, let alone pull ourselves out. It takes the grace of God and often the help of another person to get us out. But too often in life, when we see others in a pit, we regard them in a less-than-Christian manner. We may avoid helping the person for fear that it will cost us too much time, energy, or money. Or, we may sit back and judge the person who has fallen into a state of sin—or the conditions that led to it—without reaching out to the person in love.

Jesus does something different, however. He models for us what to do. He shows us how to reach out and pull our neighbor from the pit. We are called to set aside our fears and judgments about the person or situation and extend the hand of Jesus. We are called to pull our fellow travelers out of the trenches of life.

> **"Which of these three, do you think, was a neighbor to the man who fell into the hands of the robbers?" He said, "The one who showed him mercy." Jesus said to him, "Go and do likewise."**
> —LUKE 10:36–37

Nobody's Perfect

To have authenticity and consistency is not the same as being perfect! In fact, paradoxically, the first step toward authenticity and consistency is to humbly admit that we are sinners—that we have, at times, been inauthentic and inconsistent, and that we earnestly seek forgiveness so that we may become more authentic followers of Jesus.

In August 2013, Fr. Antonio Spadaro, editor of the leading Jesuit journal in Rome, asked Pope Francis the following question: "Who is Jorge Bergoglio?" The pope's answer was stunning in its simplicity and humility: "I am a sinner. This is the most accurate definition. It is not a figure of speech, a literary genre. I am a sinner." Not even the head of the Catholic Church—Christ's representative on earth who leads over one billion of the faithful throughout the world—not even he is perfect. But he sure is authentic!

In striving to present ourselves as authentic, we must follow the pope's lead. We must avoid allowing ourselves to become like the Pharisee who prayed, "God, I thank you that I am not like other people: thieves, rogues, adulterers, or even like this tax collector. I fast twice a week; I give a tenth of all my income" (Luke 18:11–12). Instead, to keep our quest for authenticity and consistency from turning into self-righteousness, we must practice humility as did the tax collector who prayed, "God, be merciful to me, a sinner" (Luke 18:13).

Luckily for us, we are born with an inclination for the truth; it is being phony that is unnatural. The *Catechism of the Catholic Church* reminds us, "Man tends by nature toward the truth" (no. 2467). In fact, to experience truth is to experience God, since Jesus said, "I am the way, and the truth, and the life" (John 14:6). To be authentic is to be holy—to be one with God who is the truth. However, to live according to the truth—to be authentic—requires vigilance. In his book *Be Yourself, Everyone Else is Already Taken*, motivational speaker and author Mike Robbins explains that despite our desire to live authentically, most of us don't, because we have been conditioned to seek the acceptance and approval of others. He emphasizes that overcoming these tendencies requires conscious effort.

As catechists, we strive to live a conscious life that is consistent with the gospel of Jesus Christ. When Jesus calls us to "Be perfect, therefore, as your heavenly Father is perfect" (Matthew 5:48), he is calling us to be authentic as God is authentic. God's authenticity can be heard in his response to Moses, who wanted to know what name God preferred. "I AM WHO I AM," was God's reply (Exodus 3:13–14)—in other words, "I am authentically God." Jesus calls us in a similar way to be authentically who *we* are as people made in the image of an authentic God.

> **"God, be merciful to me, a sinner!"**
> —Luke 18:13

I Want to Be in that Number, When the Saints Go Marching In!

The saints that we honor in our Catholic faith serve as companions on the journey of life precisely because they have walked the same roads as we do today. Like us, they had to choose whether to live a simple life faithful to God's commands or the high life of wealth, prestige, and power. Some saints, such as St. Thérèse of Lisieux, found that the path to holiness lay not in performing extraordinary deeds but in practicing small and easily overlooked acts of selflessness. In a sense, the saints put "legs" on the gospel: they show us what it means to live a Christian life in word and deed. The saints did sin and were tempted to sin just like us, but they "hit the mark" in striving to live out the Christian ideal more often than not.

In fact, the word *sin* is literally translated from Hebrew as "missing the mark." How many times in life have we tried to live a holy and perfect life, only to have our efforts go wide or fall short? More times than we can remember. What is so remarkable about the saints is that, in spite of "missing the mark" time and time again, they converted themselves each day to Christ. Over time, they conformed their will to the Father's, and in this way, by the grace of God, they became saints.

Choosing from the Menu

Catholic spirituality offers a full menu of exercises designed to help us keep it real—in other words, to be authentic. You'll find a few of those exercises on the following pages.

A catechist got his classroom set up and then went outside to gather his students, noticing that the group had surrounded a dog. Concerned that the students might be hurting the dog, he went over and asked, "What are you doing with that dog?" One of the students replied, "This dog is just an old neighborhood stray. We all want him, but only one of us can take him home. So we've decided that whoever can tell the biggest lie will get to keep the dog." Of course, the catechist was disappointed. "You kids shouldn't be having a contest telling lies!" he exclaimed. "Didn't I teach you that it's a sin to lie? Why, when I was your age, I never told a lie." There was dead silence for about a minute. Just as the catechist was beginning to think he'd gotten through to them, one of the students gave a deep sigh and said, "All right, give him the dog."

➕ **Spiritual Direction or Companionship**   Nothing helps us keep it real like another human being can! A spiritual director is a trained individual who walks with us as we discover God's presence, action, and direction in our own life. The best spiritual directors listen to us and allow us to disclose our innermost thoughts and feelings in total confidence and trust. Spiritual direction is a way for us to grow closer to God. Since God communicates with each person uniquely, it often helps to express what we hear from God through our own lives to another person. The spiritual director listens and then gives feedback about what the Holy Spirit may be up to in our life. This feedback is for our consideration only; the spiritual director is not spiritual dictator. Spiritual direction has been part of the Christian tradition for centuries, and today, many catechists are discovering it as a valuable tool for deepening their faith and their awareness of God. To locate a spiritual director near you, visit Spiritual Directors International (www.sdiworld.org).

➕ **The Daily Examen**   St. Ignatius of Loyola developed a simple method by which you can review each day in order to keep it real. This practice, known as the Daily Examen, consists of several simple steps that can be practiced in about fifteen minutes.

> First, relax in God's presence and be aware of and thankful for how God shows his love for you. Ask the Holy Spirit to come into your heart and help you look honestly at your actions and attitudes.

> Review the events of the day, recalling concrete details and particular moments from home, work, and play. Give thanks to God for these gifts.

> Once again, review the events of the day, asking yourself when you were conscious of God's presence. Express gratitude for moments when you freely chose to live as an authentic follower of Jesus.

> Express sorrow for the times you failed to be authentic in your discipleship and ask God for his abundant mercy.

> Finally, ask God for the grace and guidance you need in the day ahead to keep it real.

➕ **The Sacrament of Penance and Reconciliation**   People who are in recovery from an addiction and participate in a twelve-step program recognize the necessity of keeping it real. In fact, participants in Alcoholics Anonymous commonly assert that sobriety is 10 percent about alcohol and 90 percent about honesty. Participants know that real healing cannot and will not happen until a person stands up in front of a group of people and "names the sin." In Catholic spirituality, this kind of honesty has been facilitated through the Sacrament of Penance and Reconciliation, otherwise known as going to confession. The reason we confess to a priest is to keep it real–to name the sin out loud to another person who represents not only the healing grace and forgiveness of God, but also the church, since our sins are never private. To call others to embrace Christ means that we must embrace Christ ourselves; likewise, we cannot call others to repentance and confession if we ourselves do not repent and confess.

✚ **Ongoing Catechist Formation**   At the many workshops and presentations we hold across the country, it is not uncommon for us to encounter people who have served as catechists for forty, fifty, or even sixty years! Even more amazing is that such experienced people are attending a workshop or seminar! For catechists, one of the most effective means of keeping it real is by engaging in ongoing formation. The more we continue to learn about our faith, the better we will grow at conforming ourselves to Christ–the ultimate model of authenticity–on a daily basis.

Keeping It Real

In my book *7 Keys to Spiritual Wellness*, I describe the first and most important key to spiritual wellness as "seeing yourself as you really are." In essence, unless we have a clear perception of who we are, warts and all, we run the risk of falling prey to the deadly sin of pride. We need to keep it real. Catholic spirituality is designed to help us keep it real. We begin the Mass with the penitential rite during which we admit our sinfulness not only to God but also to one another. This is an act of humility, which is not a beating up of oneself but an exercise in recognizing that God is God and we are not.   –Joe

The Prince with a Crooked Back

The following fable is a good metaphor for what God does for us through ongoing formation: Once upon a time, there was a prince who had many riches but suffered from a crooked back that forced him to walk hunched over. His father, saddened to see his son depressed over his condition, arranged to have a sculptor erect a statue of his son. The sculpture was an exact replica of the son except for one feature: the figure in the statue had a straight back. Every day, the prince studied the statue, gazing at it for endless hours. People started to notice that, little by little, the prince was walking with a more erect gait. After a long time, the king looked out his window one day and saw the prince gazing at the statue as usual. However, as the prince began to walk away from the statue, the king and all those in the square noticed in amazement that the prince's back was no longer bent and he was no longer walking hunched over.

Throughout our lives as catechists, let us pray for the grace we need to study Jesus endlessly so that we may pattern our lives after him, the authentic Son of God. Let us also pray that we continue to "put on" Christ, our most suitable clothing, as we traverse the challenging and ever-changing terrain of life.

Questions for Reflection

> What is something you purchased recently that attracted you because of its authenticity? What is something you chose not to purchase or give your money to because you perceived it as phony?

> Who do you consider a good example of authenticity and consistency in a life of faith? What are the hallmarks of this person's life?

> In what areas of your life are you experiencing tension between who you are and what you do? How do you reconcile this tension?

> When it comes to being a catechist, do you feel a harmony between who you are and what you do? If not, what is causing the disharmony? How might you resolve it?

> What is one church teaching with which you feel a sense of discomfort or disagreement? How might you become more comfortable with this teaching?

> What can you do or say to help those you teach see your faith as authentic?

> When was a time that your authenticity showed through to those you were teaching? How did you know? How did your students react to you? What was most powerful about this experience?

> How can the Sacrament of Penance and Reconciliation help you grow in authenticity and consistency?

> Who provides a good example of humility in your life? How can you emulate this person?

> What type of ongoing formation will you do this year to help you conform to Christ and become a more authentic disciple?

For Further Reflection

Reflect on Pope Benedict XVI's remarks to the bishops of Costa Rica on how catechists are called to live what they preach: "Unite the transmission of right doctrine with personal testimony, with the firm commitment to live according to the commandments of the Lord and with the lived experience of being faithful and active members of the Church."

Spiritual Exercises

The following spiritual exercises are designed to help you develop authenticity and consistency as a person of faith. Whenever possible, practice one or more of them.

> Pray the Daily Examen once a day. (See page 52.)

> Pray the Jesus Prayer (also called the Prayer of the Heart) at the beginning of each day and at various times throughout the day: "Lord Jesus Christ, Son of God, have mercy on me, a sinner." Synchronize the prayer with your breathing: breathe in while calling out to God ("Lord, Jesus Christ, Son of God") and breathe out while praying for mercy ("have mercy on me, a sinner"). Repeat the prayer as often as you like over a period of five or ten minutes. Pray slowly, pausing between each recitation.

> Choose an opportunity to go to confession in the days or weeks ahead. Before you do so, pray an examination of conscience such as the one found at the Loyola Press website (www.loyolapress.com/an-examination-of-conscience).

> A simple prayer formula that works beautifully for children and adults alike is the "Whoops, Wow, Please, and Thank You" formula. At the end of the day, use it to reflect on the events of the day.

1. Where was your "whoops" moment today—the moment you recognized that you were being less than charitable and Christ-like in your thoughts and actions? Take some time to reflect on the situation, your feelings, and your actions during this moment in time.

2. Where was your "wow" moment today? How did this moment make you feel more alive, more loving, and more Christ-like?

3. Where was your "please" moment? What did you ask God to help you with? Did you make the request with a contrite heart? What is your petition for today? What is your petition for tomorrow?

4. End with a prayer of "thanks." Express gratitude for this day and for every day that has been given to you. Ask God to help you remember that life is a precious gift and each day an opportunity to contemplate the world with fresh eyes.

> There is a poem that became incredibly popular among youth and young adults after World Youth Day 2013, held in Rio de Janeiro, Brazil. The poem, which was incorrectly attributed to Pope Francis, appears to be have been written anonymously by someone who was inspired deeply by the message of St. John Paul II. As you read the poem, register your thoughts and attitudes. Notice which saints come to mind as models of authenticity. Notice also what people in your own life come to mind.

We Need Saints

We need saints without veil or cassock.
We need saints who wear jeans and sneakers.

We need saints who go to the movies,
listen to music and hang out with friends.

We need saints who put God in first place,
but who let go of their power.

We need saints who have time every day to pray
and who know how to date in purity and chastity,
or who consecrate their chastity.

We need modern saints, Saints of the 21st century
with a spirituality that is part of our time.

We need saints committed to the poor
and the necessary social changes.

We need saints who live in the world and who are sanctified in
*   the world,*
who are not afraid to live in the world.

We need saints who drink Coke and eat hot dogs, who wear jeans,
who are Internet-savvy, who listen to CDs.

We need saints who passionately love the Eucharist
and who are not ashamed to drink a soda or eat pizza on
*   weekends with friends.*

We need saints who like movies, the theater, music, dance, sports.

We need saints who are social, open, normal,
friendly, happy, and who are good companions.

We need saints who are in the world
and know how to taste the pure and nice things of the world
but who aren't of the world.

> Pray this short prayer asking God to inspire in you a desire for authenticity. Breathe slowly and deeply, noticing any thoughts or feelings that come to mind.

Loving God,
Instill and inspire in me a desire for honesty and authenticity in
*   all that I say and do.*
Open my eyes to see the beauty of your abundance all around me.
Open my ears to listen sincerely to those who need someone
*   to hear them.*
Open my heart to the possibilities that each moment holds
to be Christ to your people.
Amen.

What Catechists Are Saying about Consistency and Authenticity

❝I try to be a real person and not a phony. I try to do the Examen every night before I go to bed and, when I can, I go on an Ignatian retreat, which helps me talk the talk and walk the walk as a catechist. Seeing my father prepare for his confession during the sacrament of the sick during his final days on earth was touching, as well as my mom and I leaving the room for Fr. Mark to help my dad get ready for his eventual trip to heaven.   *—Lisa*

I find when I talk about prayer in my class that I feel most authentic. I talk about my personal experience in praying and the kids really seem to listen.
—Deb

Whenever I am talking to the class and I bring in personal experiences, you would be able to hear a pin drop. They know the stories are authentic; they hear it in my voice and see it in my face. The prayers we start with and end with are me talking in a personal way to God, and then the students add the Our Father. I am always conscious of the fact that I am a catechist, whether it is in class, in church, or out in public.   *—Barb*

I frequently find myself lacking that coherence, that cohesiveness I seek as a catechist, and try to return to Reconciliation occasionally. Perhaps when I am most authentic and most effective are those times when I speak to the kids about how difficult I find it to follow Christ's example and how truly awesome it is when I go to Reconciliation and receive God's forgiveness.
—Robert

I try to be mindful of the need to be authentic, because it is important to me that my students know that I "walk the talk." I do find that it is sometimes difficult. I live in a small community where I wear many hats, and I am very visible in our community. I have found that people have expectations of me because of my position (which is good for me in a way, but sometimes a little hard to live up to).   *—Nancy*

I believe being authentic is such an important part of how we can truly relate to others. We are all sinners and have faults, but in our weaknesses we have the opportunity to look at those who can help and teach us to trust in the Lord. We can also rely on our own faith to trust that the Lord will bring us through even the bumpiest of times. Authenticity is the truest way in which we can relate to others effectively, even in the imperfectness of our faults.   *—Rebecca*

There is often a tension or lack of harmony between who I am and what I do. I struggle between the wonderful life of the church (where I feel so safe) and my everyday life at work. I must say, though, that the more I learn about catechesis, the more tolerant and forgiving I become at work and even at home. I hadn't really thought about why until a couple people made comments recently. Becoming aware of this "example" has given me hope that learning more about our faith will in fact lead me to LIVING IT TOO.

–Greg

I find that the more I think with the heart and mind of Jesus, the easier decisions seem to be. I find that when I overly complicate things or try to insert "my way" into the equation, life begins to get difficult. The simplest solutions are often the easiest and asking myself two questions really helps: "What is the right and loving thing to do?" and "If Jesus were standing here in front of me would I still undertake this course of action?" These two questions have provided tremendous clarity in my desire to be authentic.

–Bernadette

I think that being authentic in ministry is revealing something of who you are. Sharing personal stories, for instance, allows people to see the humanity in the one who bears witness to Christ. I don't approach my ministry as a person of success but as a person who has far to go on the journey of life. St. Paul was a master at this. He knew that conversion is a series of beginnings. We're always starting over. We fall but by God's grace we get up again and then press on!

–Joe

At my previous job working in a group home with at-risk youth, I learned very quickly that if you are not authentic in who you are, people will recognize that, and you will lose credibility in what you are trying to accomplish. When you are being authentic, especially in ministry, your compassion, happiness, and joy naturally shine though in everything you do, which is attractive to others. I try to cultivate authenticity by praying and maintaining relationships with people who really know me and what is important to me. That way, if I am being inauthentic, they can call me out on it. **"**

–Catherine

Chapter 5

Missionary Zeal:
Fuel and Matches

Catechists should have a strong missionary spirit—a spirit that will be all the more effective if they are seen to be convinced of what they say and are enthusiastic and courageous, without ever being ashamed of the gospel.   —*Guide for Catechists*, no. 9

Campfire Cookout!

Sitting around a campfire is one of the highlights of camping trips. And planning the food to cook over the open fire is often as much fun as eating it. Whether you're frying up eggs and bacon, cooking pancakes, grilling chicken and steak, or indulging in campfire classics like s'mores and pudgy pies, food always seems to taste better when it's prepared over an open flame.

Now imagine a difference scenario. Imagine going on a camping trip and discovering that you forgot to pack matches or fire starters. You are miles from the nearest store. Instead of burgers and dogs, dinner will consist of cold beans and potato chips. Can you hear the complaints and groans of disappointment from your ravenous family members or fellow campers? And it's not just about the food. The prospect of sitting around a campsite without a blazing fire is less than exciting. Not only does the fire provide a vital source of heat on cool evenings and a means of cooking tasty food, but it creates an ambience that inspires the telling of stories, the sharing of memories, and the robust singing of songs. No overnight adventure should be experienced without a campfire!

In order to start a fire for cooking, staying warm, or telling stories, a backpacker needs a reliable source of fuel and matches. And so does the catechist. As catechists, we are called to be "on fire" for Christ so that we can nurture and grow the spark of faith in others. More than anything else, it is that spark of fire that animates our work as catechists and inspires us to be more engaging, more dynamic, and more spirit-filled. Fortunately for us, this spark—this missionary zeal—is fueled by a very reliable source of fuel: the Holy Spirit.

> **As catechists, we are called to be "on fire" for Christ so that we can nurture and grow the spark of faith in others.**

The Holy Spirit and the Lonely Goats

In the years before the Second Vatican Council, two children were overheard reenacting the story of Noah's ark. Noelle (the older of the two) was recounting for her younger brother, Michael, all the animals that Noah herded onto the ark.

"There were pigs, sheep, chickens, dogs, cats, zebras, horses, elephants, lions, birds, and even the lonely goats were brought on the ark," Noelle said.

"Wait," interrupted her brother. "Say that again. What animals were brought onto the ark?"

"There were pigs, sheep, chickens, dogs, cats, zebras, horses, elephants, lions, birds, and even the lonely goats were there," Noelle repeated. When she made mention of the lonely goats, she slowed her voice and said the "lonely goats" in a very forlorn way.

"I get it," Michael said, "but why were the goats lonely when there were all these other animals on the ark?"

"I don't know," Noelle said, "but Father Bill says it all the time at Mass when we bless ourselves: in the name of the Father, and of the Son, and of the Lonely Goats. Amen!"

Before the Second Vatican Council, the Holy Spirit was referred to in English as the Holy Ghost. (The Old English word for "spirit" is *gast*.) At the council, however, the decision was made to begin referring to the Third Person of the Trinity as the Holy Spirit. This decision revived the earliest Christian understanding of God's movement in the world as breath. (The Greek word for *breath* is *pneuma*, which is why the formal study of the Holy Spirit is called *pneumatology*.) The decision also reinforced our liturgical and practical understanding of God as Spirit. During Holy Week, at the Chrism Mass, for example, the breath of the Holy Spirit is poured out as the bishop audibly and visibly breathes on the holy oils that will be used for the sacred Triduum. It is also customary in various parts of the world to leave a window open in the room where a person is dying, so that when the breath of the soul leaves the body it can escape through the window and rejoin the spirit world.

While the word *ghost* implies something that is not visible, the Holy Spirit is made visible and manifest in our lives as Christians. We may not be able to see the Holy Spirit, but we can certainly recognize the presence of the Holy Spirit.

> ## O Breathe on Me
>
> O breathe on me, O breath of God,
> fill me with life anew
> that I may love the things You love,
> and do what you would do.
> O breathe on me, O breath of God,
> until my heart is pure;
> until my will is one with Yours,
> to do and to endure.
> O breathe on me, O breath of God,
> my will to Yours incline,
> until this selfish part of me
> glows with Your fire divine.
> O breathe on me, O breath of God,
> so I shall never die,
> but live with You the perfect life
> for all eternity.
>
> —attributed to
> St. Columba of Ireland

The Holy Spirit: Putting the "Bam" in Your Life

One of the reasons that I (Julianne) love to watch cooking shows is because the personality of the chefs influences the types of food they prepare. Emeril Lagasse, for example, has a passion for food, and this passion shows through in the way he talks about food, prepares his food, and presents his food. One of his trademarks is to exclaim "BAM!" when he puts his special spice blend in his food or when he presents his final meal for consideration. This makes me laugh out loud!

I like to think of the Holy Spirit as the divine chef that puts spiritual spice in the ordinary food of our lives and transforms it into something special, something unique, something we can't help but take notice of. BAM!

We Didn't Start the Fire!

Whether he intended it or not, we can thank Billy Joel for one of the catchiest tunes that applies to the Holy Spirit. His song "We Didn't Start the

Fire" exclaims that a fire we didn't start has been burning as long as the world has been turning. What a great metaphor for the Christian life: a life fueled by the power, energy, and dynamism of the Holy Spirit.

It is the Holy Spirit who inflames our hearts as catechists and whose divine energy created the heavens from nothingness. The Holy Spirit is ever moving, dynamic, and active. It is the Holy Spirit who calls us, propels us forward in our faith, and inspires us to

"A man from 'Ripley's Believe It or Not!' wants a picture of someone on fire for the Lord."

The Forgotten God

The Holy Spirit has often been called "the forgotten God" when it comes to the Persons of the Trinity and yet, throughout Scripture, the Holy Spirit is the catalyst for a missionary zeal that is marked by great joy, courage, and boldness.

> The prophet Jeremiah speaks of this zeal when he says, "If I say, 'I will not mention him, or speak any more in his name', then within me there is something like a burning fire shut up in my bones; I am weary with holding it in, and I cannot" (Jeremiah 20:9).

> The two disciples on the road to Emmaus speak of this zeal when they say, "Were not our hearts burning within us while he was talking to us on the road?" (Luke 24:32).

> Peter and John refer to this zeal when they tell the Sanhedrin, "We cannot keep from speaking about what we have seen and heard" (Acts of the Apostles 4:20).

> St. Paul alludes to this zeal when he says, "Woe to me if I do not proclaim the gospel!" (1 Corinthians 9:16).

All these witnesses to the Holy Spirit speak of such a burning desire to share the Word of God that they can't keep it in. Nor should they— or we! The best gifts are not meant to be kept secret or hidden away, but to be shared freely.

A catechist was seeing her students off after class when one of them said, "That was a really good class, Mrs. Martinez," to which she replied, "Oh, I have to give all the credit to the Holy Spirit!" The student then replied, "It wasn't THAT good!"

form those we teach. Our vocation, faith, and inspiration do not come from our own efforts, but rather from our communion with the Holy Spirit who nourishes and sustains us. It is the Holy Spirit who will renew the face of the earth and keep the fire burning "on, and on, and on," as Billy Joel sings, long after we are gone.

The Holy Spirit makes different gifts freely available to each one of us. These gifts help each of us live a holy life—not a rigidly pious life, but one full of passion and zeal—and inspire similar living in others. One of the simplest ways we can do this is by speaking with conviction. If we are convinced by what we say, and if we look as though we are convinced by what we say, people will pay close attention to us. They will hear the Word of God that crosses our lips and has clearly changed our lives.

Catechists with a true vocation take our baptismal call to proclaim God's Word to the next level. Our desire to share Christ with others is powerful, almost overwhelming. We can't help but preach the gospel to others! To keep the flame burning, we nurture our spirituality through an active prayer life and ongoing formation that keeps us fresh and enthusiastic about our relationship with the Lord. The flip side of our desire to proclaim the Word of God, after all, is an unquenchable desire to keep learning about the Word of God ourselves. As catechists, we never stop learning!

Me, an Evangelist?

What do you think about when you hear the word *evangelization*? Does it call to mind images of popular televangelists? A knock at the door from someone who asks you if you have accepted Jesus Christ as

> I wish that all were as I myself am. But each has a particular gift from God, one having one kind and another a different kind.
> —1 Corinthians 7:7

your Lord and Savior? Maybe it has become synonymous in your mind with sending money overseas to children who have never heard of Christ. If any of these things crossed your mind, you are certainly not alone. When we think of evangelization, however, we should actually think of one person and one person only: Jesus Christ.

Our word *evangelism* comes from the Greek word *euangelizomai*, which literally means "to bring good news." The Good News that we bring to the world when we evangelize is not only the message of Jesus Christ but the person of Jesus Christ, who desires a personal relationship with each one of us. It is this personal relationship that lies at the heart of evangelization, in which we are all called to encounter Christ, to deepen the encounter with Christ over a lifetime, and to introduce others to Christ. As the *Catechism of the Catholic Church* reminds us, "the loving knowledge of Christ springs out of the irresistible desire to announce, to evangelize, and to lead others to the 'yes' of the faith in Jesus Christ." Tapping into the power of the Holy Spirit helps us introduce Christ to others and deepen our own faith as well.

But What If I'm an Introvert?

Being on fire with the Holy Spirit does not mean that you have to begin speaking about your faith with a megaphone, especially if you are the quiet type or even an introvert. Remember what we said in the last chapter about authenticity? One of the unfortunate realities of Christianity is the proliferation of media "evangelists" who seek to convince their viewers of their zeal by speaking loudly and quickly and with very high energy but end up coming across as phony. They don't realize that passion and zeal can also be subtle realities. In her book *Quiet Influence: The Introvert's Guide to Making a Difference,* author Jennifer B. Kahnweiler, Ph.D., explains that we do not necessarily need fiery words or dramatic body language to express passion. In fact, Kahnweiler asserts, we live in a time when people have grown weary of in-your-face salesmanship and are looking for a more personal connection.

> **For Christ did not send me to baptize but to proclaim the gospel, and not with eloquent wisdom, so that the cross of Christ might not be emptied of its power.**
> —1 Corinthians 1:17

So, then, how can we catechists show our missionary zeal in ways that are authentic, personal, and not off-putting? Let's take a look at several strategies.

➕ **Make sure the fire is coming from deep within.** Paradoxically, missionary zeal is fueled by withdrawing into solitude on a regular basis. Jesus most definitely had missionary zeal. And yet, time and again, Scripture tells us that he withdrew to a quiet place to pray in solitude. If we are going to show passion for the Good News, we need to begin by sitting quietly in solitude from time to time and allowing the Good News to permeate the very core of our being.

➕ **Show your passion by thoroughly planning and preparing your lessons.** We can show our excitement and zeal for the Good News of Jesus by paying attention to the details of our lessons. A creative, well-planned lesson shows those we teach that catechesis is a priority in our lives; it shows them that we're not just "phoning it in." Recall the scene from the classic movie *It's a Wonderful Life*, for example, in which George Bailey and his new wife, Mary, abruptly cancel their honeymoon because of the bank crisis. After a long day at the bank, George receives a call from Mary telling him to meet her at their "honeymoon suite," which turns out to be the old abandoned building he and Mary once dreamed of transforming into their home. As George enters the old dilapidated house, he is astounded to see how much effort Mary has expended to make this event special: a candlelight dinner has been laid, travel posters are pasted up everywhere, makeshift drapes hang in the windows, their friends Bert and Ernie are serenading outside, and a chicken is roasting on a spit in the fireplace. Mary doesn't say a word as George enters, but her preparations leave no room for doubt about her passion! As catechists, we can communicate our own passion and zeal for the Lord by our attention to detail as we prepare and plan for the session we are about to lead. Likewise, when students ask questions and we are prepared with an informed answer, we communicate our passion and zeal for our own faith formation. This double example is a powerful one.

➕ **Show your zeal by giving others your undivided attention** Once, as I (Joe) was making my way through an airport, I spied a scene in which a young girl—maybe two years of age—was balancing herself precariously on a horizontal pole and calling out, "Mommy, look! Mommy, Mommy, look! Look at me, Mommy! Mommy, look!" With their children's help, parents learn very early on that their greatest responsibility and one of the greatest gifts they can offer their child is their undivided attention. Similarly, one of the most effective ways we as catechists can show missionary zeal is by devoting our undivided attention to those we are evangelizing as we listen to their stories, questions, concerns, and insights. A major mistake that many Christians make when evangelizing, however, is doing all the talking and calling attention to themselves. The temptation is to show enthusiasm for the gospel by speaking endlessly and with great enthusiasm. But while endless speaking is a turn-off, listening builds trust. And when people trust, they are open to being led. Branding and marketing guru Tom Asacker tells his audiences that people aren't interested in you, but they want you to be interested in them; they want you to show them how their association with you will positively impact their lives. As catechists, we can show others, through our interest in them and our undivided attention, that their association with us—and ultimately with Jesus—will have a downright heavenly impact on them and their lives.

He Descended into Hell

A high school student once confided in me that he had tried to take his own life because he was being bullied relentlessly. He described his life as a living hell. Hoping to bring him a small measure of comfort, I gave him a prayer card that depicted Jesus standing on a split rock, reaching down to save those in hell. I explained to him that in the Apostles' Creed, we recite the phrase "he descended into hell" for a reason: there is no hell that we can experience in our own lives that Christ has not experienced before us; there is no suffering and no pain that Christ has not suffered first. Many years later, this former student shared with me that he still carries the prayer card in his wallet as a reminder that he is never alone, even in the darkest moments of his life.

—Julianne

✚ **Go one-on-one.** Evangelizing need not consist of rousing speeches delivered to huge crowds. We can show our enthusiasm and zeal for the gospel by engaging people in one-on-one situations that enable us to address individual concerns and needs. True, Jesus spoke to vast crowds on several occasions, but he also had numerous encounters with people one-on-one. We can show our missionary zeal by seeking out opportunities to have meaningful conversations with the individuals we teach.

✚ **Connect with others through the written word and through images.** Words do not always have to be spoken out loud in order to convey passion and zeal. Sending someone a note, a card, an e-mail, a text message, or a tweet that contains thoughtful words and an inspiring image can communicate to the person just how passionate you are about their well-being.

✚ **Show your passion through calmness.** The central message of Christianity is that sin and death have been defeated and that we have nothing to fear. This certainly gives rise to joy, but it also gives rise to contentment. One of the ways Christians can show a zeal for the gospel is by exhibiting a calmness that says, "Deep in my heart, I truly believe that all shall be well." People are drawn to leaders who exhibit calm in the midst of chaos. As catechists, our job is not to put the fear of hell into our students but to invite them to walk with Jesus, who calms the storms of our lives.

College basketball coaching legend John Wooden said that "highs lead to lows" and that while "swings of intensity result in instability," "quiet enthusiasm gets results." Our missionary zeal need not be loud and noisy. Our "quiet enthusiasm," however, can get the job done.

Bringing Missionary Zeal to Today's Mission Fields

Do you remember hearing people talk about sending help to "the missions"? In decades past, this meant gathering money or clothing for people overseas, in the poorest countries of the world. While the Catholic Church still does plenty of outreach in such countries, we are also called to be mindful of the mission fields that are all around us.

Our local community is our most immediate mission field. As catechists, we may meet people who do not know the basic story of the life, death, and resurrection of Christ. Many children in our own neighborhoods may not know how to make the sign of the cross or how to use a Bible.

Many adults in our communities may have heard the basic message of Christ but mistakenly believe that it has nothing of value to offer them. For all these reasons and more, our mission field has shifted from a foreign to a domestic one. Being a catechist means that you are sensitive to this. It means that the whole world is your classroom and that every encounter is an opportunity to be Christ and proclaim Christ in word and witness.

Pope Francis emphasizes this idea in his encyclical *Evangelii Gaudium*. He encourages us to be disciples-on-the-go, ready to bring the love of Christ to others in the ordinary and extraordinary moments of our lives. "Being a disciple means being constantly ready to bring the love of Jesus to others," he writes, "and this can happen unexpectedly and in any place: on the street, in a city square, during work, on a journey."

For many young people today, religion is seen as one option among many. They may never pick up the Gospels or encounter Christ through the beauty of the Mass. But as Catholics who immerse ourselves in the Word, we are called to *be* the gospel in the world. The Scriptures are to be writ large in our lives so that all those we meet encounter Christ in who we are and in the love we extend to them. Just as Jesus made the hearts of the disciples burn on the road to Emmaus, so we, in word and in example, are called to "warm hearts" through our proclamation of the good news.

> **Are we still a Church capable of warming hearts?**
> —Pope Francis

Someone Else Needs the Wood

There is a humorous expression that I (Julianne) have often heard repeated when someone is whining—or, as they say in Ireland, "whinging"—about their situation: "Get down off the cross, someone else needs the wood!" This expression reminds us that our sufferings grow small when we begin to count our blessings and to consider what Christ went through for each one of us. This doesn't mean that we should minimize the suffering of others, but that we should remember that the sadness of Good Friday is always followed by the joy of Resurrection on Easter Sunday. Each of us will experience trials and tribulations in life, but because Christ has gone before us and triumphed over sin and death, the road ahead is much greater than the path behind.

As catechists, we need to remember that the Jesus we so zealously desire to preach is the crucified *and* the risen Christ. We should not allow our zeal to blind us to the sufferings of those we teach. Instead, it should bind us to them in fraternal love as we seek to alleviate their suffering however we can. Yes, we preach the Good News of new life in Christ, but we do so knowing that this new life comes through suffering and death. This awareness might be expressed in a kind word, by uplifting a student in fervent prayer, by reaching out with a home-cooked meal, by sending a card or a note, or through the ministry of our presence. Simple gestures like these make Christ visible during the most difficult moments of people's lives. Helping someone connect their suffering to Christ's and their individual story to the larger story of God's faithfulness is a tremendous gift. Indeed, it is the most precious gift that can be offered in a time of grief and sadness.

Our approach should not be dour and somber, but empathetic and patient. Two of the greatest evangelists the world has known were marked by their great sense of joy, peace, and holy presence. Think about the face of Blessed Teresa as she touched the wounds of the "untouchables" in the slums of Calcutta, or the face of St. John Paul II as he embraced the cross of suffering from Parkinson's disease. The light of the Holy Spirit was clearly evident on their faces, but their pain was no less real. Instead, the love of Christ, through the power of the Holy Spirit, transfigured their suffering. Recalling this can help us be more loving, more kind, and more patient with those who suffer, even if we are suffering ourselves. Just as the heat from a fire warms all those who sit around it, so too does the zeal of the Holy Spirit radiate from one person to another.

Questions for Reflection

> Reflect on your understanding of the word *zeal*. How do you exhibit zeal in your life?
> Who in your life radiates zeal in all they say and do? What do they teach you about zeal?

> Do you consider yourself to be a missionary disciple? Why or why not?
> What do you do to keep the fire of the Holy Spirit burning within you?
> Are you an introvert or an extrovert? How can you show passion and zeal and remain authentic?
> How do you express passion and zeal without using words?
> When was a time that someone gave you undivided attention when you needed it most? What images come to mind when you think of the Holy Spirit? What people come to mind when you think of the Holy Spirit?
> In what ways do you feel that you embody the Holy Spirit?
> The Holy Spirit has often been called the "forgotten God." Why do you think this is so? How can you call upon the power of the Holy Spirit each day in your life?

For Further Reflection

"The New Evangelization is a time of awakening, of new encouragement and new witness that Jesus Christ is the center of our faith and daily life. It calls on every member of the Church to a renewal of faith and an actual effort to share it."

—The Synod of Bishops on the New Evangelization for the Transmission of the Christian Faith, Proposition 5

Spiritual Exercises

The following spiritual exercises will help you fan the flames of your missionary zeal through the power and inspiration of the Holy Spirit. Reflect on the following exercises. Consider sharing the fruits of those you practice with a friend or a fellow catechist.

> Following is a list of attributes of the Holy Spirit. After reading them, let your heart rest in the characteristic of the Holy Spirit that most speaks to your heart. Open your Bible and read the passage that applies to this attribute. Reflect on the passage and on your call to be a catechist. Take some notes, then stop and ask the Holy Spirit to be with you in this moment. Think of a specific intention that you would like help with. Ask the Holy Spirit to help you with this intention and say a prayer of gratitude for all your blessings.

The Holy Spirit as . . .

- teacher of truth (John 14:6)
- prayer partner (Romans 8:26)
- helper in holiness (2 Peter 1:16, 1 Corinthians 6:19-20, James 4:7, 2 Timothy 2:21)
- protector in peril (Ephesians 6:10-17)
- liberator from sin (1 Corinthians 6:11)
- maker of new people in Christ (2 Corinthians 5:17)
- source of service (Romans 12:3-8, 1 Corinthians 12, 1 Peter 4:11)
- trainer of evangelists (Matthew 5:13-14, 28:19-20; Acts of the Apostles 1:8; Isaiah 55:11; Mark 13:11)
- counselor in times of confusion (John 10:4)

> Read and reflect on the poem "God's Grandeur" by Gerard Manley Hopkins in a peaceful place of your choosing. Whether outdoors or indoors, the setting should allow you to relax and reflect on the world and your place in it. Underline the phrase or sentence that speaks most to you. Call to mind someone in your life who embodies the "flame" of the Holy Spirit and give thanks for that person.

The world is charged with the grandeur of God.
It will flame out, like shining from shook foil;
It gathers to a greatness, like the ooze of oil
Crushed. Why do men then now not reck his rod?
Generations have trod, have trod, have trod;
And all is seared with trade; bleared, smeared with toil;
And wears man's smudge and shares man's smell: the soil
Is bare now, nor can foot feel, being shod.

And for all this, nature is never spent;
here lives the dearest freshness deep down things;
And though the last lights off the black West went
Oh, morning, at the brown brink eastward, springs–
Because the Holy Ghost over the bent
World broods with warm breast and with ah! bright wings.

> Pray the following prayer to the Holy Spirit. Ask that the Holy Spirit increase your faith and inspire you more deeply in your vocation as a catechist.

V. Come, Holy Spirit, fill the hearts of your faithful
R. And kindle in me the fire of your love.
V. Send forth your Spirit, so that I shall be created.
R. And you shall renew the face of the earth.
O, God, by the light of the Holy Spirit
you have taught the hearts of your faithful.
In the same Spirit,
help us to know what is truly right and always to rejoice
    in your consolation.
We ask this through Christ, Our Lord.   Amen.

> Reflect on the gifts of the Holy Spirit: wisdom, understanding, knowledge, counsel, fortitude, piety, and fear of the Lord. Which gifts do you feel you have been given? Which gifts have deepened over time? Which gifts do you feel have not been given to you?

> Reflect on the fruits of the Holy Spirit: charity, joy, peace, patience, kindness, goodness, generosity, gentleness, faithfulness, modesty, self-control, and chastity. Focus on one or two fruits. What person in your life has most embodied this fruit or fruits? How did they share it with you? What faith lessons did you learn from this person?

> In her famous prayer "Christ Has No Body," St. Theresa of Avila (1515–1582) teaches us how to bring the Holy Spirit alive for those we encounter. As you pray, let your mind linger on the phrase or word that most resonates with you. Ponder in your heart why this phrase or word speaks to you. What message of hope from the Holy Spirit does it hold for you?

Christ has no body but yours,
No hands, no feet on earth but yours,
Yours are the eyes with which he looks
Compassion on this world,
Yours are the feet with which he walks to do good,
Yours are the hands, with which he blesses all the world.
Yours are the hands, yours are the feet,
Yours are the eyes, you are his body.
Christ has no body now but yours,
No hands, no feet on earth but yours,
Yours are the eyes with which he looks
compassion on this world.
Christ has no body now on earth but yours.

What Catechists Are Saying about Missionary Zeal

❝I always thought that a missionary was a religious or a priest sent overseas to a remote country of the world. I never thought of myself this way until I heard Pope Francis talk about how each of us is a missionary by virtue of our baptism. My missionary journey began sixteen years ago when I was asked to be a second-grade catechist. Through these sixteen years I am hopeful that I have made an impact on the lives of the children in my parish. My mission wasn't to a remote location, but to my home town, and it is one that I have never once regretted.   *−Claire*

I have always prayed to the Holy Spirit and have felt very alive in the Holy Spirit throughout my life. I have a very passionate nature—I am half Italian and half Spanish, and neither nation is known for producing wallflowers. But as a young adult, I found myself praying to be more quiet, reserved, and reticent, as I wanted to be seen as being more responsible and serious. I particularly admired the Adult Faith Formation leader at my parish, Sr. Diane. She always seemed to be the epitome of calmness and peace. Her voice was soothing and her presence enveloping. I wanted to have that sense of peace in my life and not this wild energy that I had been given. So, I prayed to become more like Sr. Diane. One day I happened to mention this to Sr. Diane and she laughed! But she also told me that I shouldn't pray to be more like someone else but to ask the Holy Spirit to increase the gifts that I have been given and the desire to use them for God's purposes. I realized that the gifts that I had been given by the Holy Spirit were good and that instead of comparing myself to anyone else, I should focus on increasing the gifts I was given and tempering those less than attractive qualities within myself.   *−Jane*

I add "zest" to my recipes in baking quite a lot. The fresh burst of citrus added to a muffin or scone can make all the difference. I like to think that this is what zeal does—it adds that little burst of freshness to everything that we taste. For me, having missionary zeal means that I can bring something bright and fresh to the world, inspired by the Holy Spirit.   *−Pam*

I need to do a better job of connecting with the Holy Spirit. I realize that in my prayer life I do a lot of talking to God rather than listening to what the Spirit is asking of me and showing me.   *−Frank*

On Pentecost, a priest at our parish said, "You have to be hungry!" He meant we have to hunger for the Holy Spirit, the Fruits, and the Gifts.

St. Theresa, in her joy, still hungered, didn't she? Her sadness, doubt, and anxieties were a hunger, were they not? —*Kathy*

A favorite prayer of mine is "Come Holy Spirit, fill the hearts of your faithful and enkindle in them the fire of your love. Send forth your spirit and they shall be created and you shall renew the face of the earth." I like to invite the Holy Spirit before each of my Religious Ed classes. —*Carla*

The Holy Spirit guides us, leads us, and helps us to change from the inside out. He has helped me become the new creation that Christ died for me to become. He is gentle yet firm and always here. He is tender and loving. Ask for his filling and anointing. —*Donna*

There is a tremendous need for more teaching on the Holy Spirit so believers, new and old, can understand on a deeper, more personal level, truly enjoy walking in the Spirit all the time, and just enjoy the constant presence of the Holy Spirit dwelling within them. It's a wonderful thing to grasp. It completely changed my personal walk with the Lord when I gained a clearer understanding of the grace, the Spirit, and the love of God. These subjects need to be taught more and more. —*Cassie*

We need the Holy Spirit to ferociously blow us in directions we may not want to go. We need him to carry us along in the strong currents that take us to his place of operation: the place where he wants us to be. 🗩 —*Michael*

Chapter 6

Devotion to Mary and the Saints: Flashlight and Batteries

> "The spirituality of catechists, like that of every Christian and especially those involved in the apostolate, will be enriched by a deep devotion to the Mother of God." —*Guide for Catechists*, no. 10

When the Path Becomes Murky

A number of years ago, I (Joe) went camping with a friend and left the tent at night to find my way to the car to get something I had left in the trunk. After I had walked about fifty feet down a winding path, I realized that I was completely enveloped in darkness. I couldn't see in front of me or behind me, to the right or to the left, or up or down, for that matter. Why hadn't I taken a flashlight with me, you ask? Because that was the object I was going to retrieve from the car!

At times, it may grow so dark at a campsite or along the path that a backpacker needs to shed a little light by way of a reliable flashlight with fresh batteries. Catechists, too, recognize that sometimes, the spiritual path becomes murky and difficult to discern. Luckily, we have reliable sources of light—Mary and the saints—who brighten the path to Jesus and make it visible so we don't stumble or lose our way.

A Living Catechism

You may have heard the expression "Faith is taught but also caught." This is true; we human beings learn by imitation. As catechists, we can become more effective religious educators by modeling our teaching style on that of those whom we admire and respect. We can incorporate their techniques into our own repertoire and borrow elements of their teaching style to develop an approach that is personal and authentic but also well-informed by those who have gone before. We can look to many such models: some living, others from the past, some known only to ourselves, and others who are the great saints of the church. As catechists, we stand on the shoulders of those who have passed on the faith for two thousand years. What a legacy of faith we are part of!

> **The church lovingly and respectfully refers to Mary as a "living catechism" and as the "mother and model of catechists."**

Of all the models that we can look to, however, none stands taller than Mary, the Mother of Jesus and our Mother too. She gave Jesus life through the power of the Holy Spirit and gave us life through the gift of her Son. But Mary's role did not end after giving birth to Jesus. Mary was Jesus' first teacher, instructing him in the traditions and teachings of Judaism and in the human knowledge of Scripture. She taught him of God's plan of salvation, instilling in him the radical love of God and neighbor that would one day lead him to perform the ultimate sacrifice—the laying down of his life for those he loved. Because she enabled his Word to come alive in the world, Mary is considered the first disciple of Jesus. The church lovingly and respectfully refers to her as a "living catechism" and as the "mother and model of catechists."

This Is My Body

I (Julianne) have a priest friend named Dave. One day, Father Dave shared a delightful story about how his relationship with the Blessed Mother deepened as a result of meeting a young mother with two little children. This woman was very involved in parish life as a catechist, but during events such as in-services and retreats, she would often leave for an extended period of time. Guessing that Father Dave might be puzzled by her comings and goings, she explained to him one day that she was a nursing mother, and that whenever she was away from home for a time, her husband would bring their hungry daughter to her to be fed. Father Dave confessed that he had never thought about the level of sacrifice involved in nursing a child before.

The following Sunday, as he elevated the host, he had a moment of penetrating insight. The words *This is my body, given for you* took on a powerful significance and gave him a deeper appreciation of the Blessed Mother's self-giving. She gave her body completely over to her child. She gave him life and nourishment both inside and outside of the womb.

As we remember Jesus' words at the Last Supper—"This is my body, given for you"—we remember how Mary did the same for Jesus. We remember that in the Eucharist, Christ gives his body and blood to nourish each of us, just as Mary did for him.

Mary, the Model Catechist

The final words attributed to Mary in the New Testament are found in John's Gospel, during the wedding feast at Cana, when Mary instructs the servants to "Do whatever he tells you" (John 2:5). These are the words of a catechist: Mary is instructing others to follow Jesus' commands. Isn't this what we do too? That's why Mary is the first and best model for catechists.

> **"Do whatever he tells you."**
> —John 2:5

Another reason Mary is a model for catechists is because she faithfully contemplated the events of her life. Confronted with the mystery of God's life taking shape within and around her, Mary, we are told, "treasured all these words and pondered them in her heart" (Luke 2:19). We know that Mary was a woman of action, of course, for she set out "with haste" to visit her cousin Elizabeth and to share the good news (Luke 1:39). But we also know that Mary was a woman of contemplation. She pondered the mystery of God's grace, which then enabled her to act in confidence and faith. As catechists, we are called to contemplate—to ponder the mystery of God's grace in our lives, in our world, and in the lives of those we teach—and then to put this grace into action.

The Acts of the Apostles (1:14) tells us of the early Christian community gathering in prayer, celebrating the Eucharist, and building the community with Mary in their midst. We should do no less. The spirituality of all baptized Christians is enriched by devotion to Mary; however, as catechists, our ministry is especially enriched by devotion to the Blessed Mother.

A catechist was teaching her students about the Nativity. "Who is the mother of Jesus?" she asked. Without hesitation, the class responded in unison, "Mary!" "That's right," she answered. "Now, who can name the father of Jesus?" There was a long, quiet pause before one of the students blurted out, "I know! It's Virg!" The catechist had never gotten this as a response before and was taken by surprise. "Virg? Why would you say that?" she asked. The student responded, "Because my grandma always taught me to pray to Virg 'n' Mary 'n' the child Jesus."

Mary clearly recognized Jesus as Lord. She had a deep, abiding faith. Her heart was united with the heart of Jesus. Her life was a perfect example of living according to God's will. These are qualities we catechists seek: deep faith, union with Christ in prayer, and lives that conform to God's will. Our goal as catechists, therefore, is to emulate Mary, our Mother, asking her to bring us closer to her Son, Jesus, and to help us hear and follow the Father's call.

Our Lady of Good Help: The Comfort of Catechists

For more than 150 years, pilgrims from all over the world have visited the Shrine of Our Lady of Good Help in New Franken, Wisconsin, a quaint and peaceful sanctuary in the midst of farmland about seventeen miles from Green Bay. It was in this unassuming place that Our Lady appeared to Sr. Adele Brise, a young immigrant from Belgium, on October 9, 1859. Our Lady identified herself as follows: "I am the Queen of Heaven and I pray for the conversion of sinners." Her message to Sr. Adele was both profound and simple. "Gather the children in this wild country," she said, "and teach them what they should know for salvation. Go and fear nothing. I will help you."

A chapel and school were built in subsequent years and all people in the area, especially children, were invited to attend religious education led by Sr. Adele. The shrine became a local center of education and pilgrimage. Following the Great Peshtigo Fire of 1871, the shrine grew in importance. The fire, which remains the most devastating fire in U.S. history, killed 2,000 people and destroyed over a million acres in northeastern

Wisconsin. So powerful was this fire that it "leaped" over the Green Bay of Lake Michigan and began to progress up the Door County peninsula. People from all over the peninsula gathered at the shrine for protection and prayer. An outdoor rosary procession was held, and a statue of Our Lady was processed through the grounds. Despite the fact that the farmlands all around the shrine were scorched and many buildings reduced to ashes, the Shrine of Our Lady of Good Help, its grounds, and the people gathered there were unharmed. This phenomenon cemented the shrine's reputation as a place of miraculous healing. Indeed, many other miracles have since been attributed to Our Lady at the shrine. Visitors marvel at its walls, lined with the old crutches of those who no longer need them.

What a gift and a blessing Our Lady of Good Help is to us catechists, who seek to teach children "what they should know for salvation." Her advice is especially comforting as we strive to be the best catechists we can be despite our fears and doubts. Her words "Go and fear nothing, I will help you" are a source of comfort and refuge for catechists just as surely as is the shrine itself.

Presenting Jesus to the World

It's interesting to note that in artworks, Mary is often shown holding up the child Jesus as if presenting him to bless us. This is what we are called to do as catechists: present Jesus to the world. We can perform this basic task in many ways. Here are a few of them.

✚ When we were asked to be a catechist, our reaction was probably similar to Mary's: we may have asked, "How can this be?" Like Mary, we may have been perplexed by such a challenge. And, like Mary, we may also have responded yes in spite of our wonderment. "Here I

Approved!

On December 8, 2010, Bishop David L. Ricken of the Diocese of Green Bay formally approved the apparition to Sr. Adele. This made the Shrine of Our Lady of Good Help the first approved Marian apparition site in the United States, and only the tenth Vatican-approved Marian apparition site in the world. Today, the shrine welcomes hundreds of thousands of pilgrims each year.

am, the servant of the Lord," she said. "Let it be with me according to your word" (Luke 1:38). God responds to the humility of her yes and to ours by giving us what we need to complete the task: God does not call the qualified but qualifies the called. Like Mary, we can continually strive to say yes to God's call to embody his Son, Jesus, and to bring him to others.

> **We can continually strive to say yes to God's call to embody his Son, Jesus, and to bring him to others.**

✚ As soon as Mary found out that she was called to be the Mother of Jesus, she leapt into action. In Luke 1:38, the angel departs from her, and in the very next verse she sets out to visit her cousin Elizabeth "with haste"! We can imitate Mary by showing our missionary zeal—by moving eagerly into action to bring the good news of Jesus to others. We can stir the life that is within them as Mary's greeting stirred the baby in Elizabeth's womb.

✚ Several times in Scripture, Mary "ponders" or "treasures" things in her heart. She does so after the shepherds visit (Luke 2:19) and again after finding the child Jesus in the Temple (Luke 2:51). No doubt Mary pondered many experiences in her heart throughout her life. We can imitate Mary by being contemplative in a similar manner. When events happen in our lives, we can turn them over and over in our heart. We can review them to more readily recognize the hand of God in our everyday lives. We can then teach our students to do the same.

> **But Mary treasured all these words and pondered them in her heart.**
> —LUKE 2:19

✚ Among many Christians, especially those of Eastern traditions, the visit of the Magi, Jesus' baptism in the Jordan, and the wedding feast at Cana are seen as a threefold "epiphany," or revealing. Mary is intimately involved in two of these three events. As catechists, we can imitate Mary by making sure that our catechesis is always an "epiphany"—a revealing of Jesus' true identity. We can also imitate Mary by urging those we teach to do what Jesus asks.

➕ In the Gospel of John, Mary is said to be at the foot of the cross at the moment of Jesus' death. She is part of what is known as the "Little Company of Mary"—the small band of faithful disciples who stood nearby throughout Jesus' suffering and death. We can imitate Mary by being present to the suffering in the lives of those we teach and in the community around us. As difficult as it is to remain present when we are afraid, Mary's stoicism reminds us that God will be with us even when we are at our most broken and fearful.

➕ The Acts of the Apostles tells us that the early Christian community gathered united around Mary (1:14). Acts also tells us that "when the day of Pentecost had come, they were all together in one place" (Acts 2:1). Through the power of the Holy Spirit, Mary gave Jesus life; it makes sense, then, that she would be present at Pentecost, when his Spirit was born into the world in a new way, signifying new life for

Pondering Is *Not* Inaction

Pondering the mysteries of faith in our heart does not lead to inertia. In fact, it leads to the opposite: action and great fruit. Blessed Teresa says it best, "The fruit of silence is prayer. The fruit of prayer is faith. The fruit of faith is love. The fruit of love is service. The fruit of service is peace."

The Sisters of the Little Company of Mary

About a mile from where I live in Evergreen Park, Illinois, is Little Company of Mary Hospital. The hospital is operated by the Sisters of the Little Company of Mary, a congregation that was founded by Venerable Mary Potter in England in 1877. Its name comes from the "little company" of people who stood at the foot of the cross. The community strives to imitate Mary's motherly love for her son.

—Joe

all. Because Mary paid close attention to the promptings of the Holy Spirit throughout her life, we can trust that on the day of Pentecost she, along with the disciples, was filled with the outpouring of the Holy Spirit and sent forth to proclaim the Good News. We can imitate Mary by being Spirit-filled—by praying for the gifts and fruits of the Holy Spirit so that we may effectively proclaim Jesus' Word.

✚ Finally, we can look to Mary's Assumption as a sign of hope. When Mary's time on earth was completed, she was assumed body and soul into heaven—a precursor, so to speak, of the Resurrection of the Body that we all look forward to. Our ministry, as catechists, is grounded in hope. Mary's Assumption is a sign of hope, an invitation to wait with confidence for that day when we shall see God face-to-face, united body and soul with him for all eternity.

Mary is, indeed, a "living catechism," the "mother and model of catechists."

The Gift of Spiritual Healing

I (Julianne) had the opportunity to make a pilgrimage to Lourdes, France, a couple of years ago. I went in memory of my mother, who had passed away at age 54 from cancer. Throughout my pilgrimage I could feel the presence of both my mother and the Blessed Mother all around me.

The faith of the pilgrims in Lourdes is unlike anything that I have ever experienced. From the confession lines and those who wait for hours to go into "the baths" for healing, the atmosphere is intense and prayerful. In the evening, a candlelight rosary is recited in many different languages as the crowds pray together and walk through the grounds. The sick, the terminally ill, and children in wheelchairs are at the front of the procession. As I walked behind the pilgrims, I was reminded of Jesus' words: "So the last will be first, and the first will be last" (Matthew 20:16).

My mother had traveled to Lourdes with her two brothers shortly before her death. I have a picture of her on the steps of the basilica that I will treasure forever. Despite the ravages of her illness, she looks beautiful and radiant. We talked about this before she died, and she told me that the gift she had received in Lourdes was not one of physical healing, but of spiritual healing. She felt that Mary had given her a deep sense of peace so that she would be ready to meet her Son in death.

A deep sense of peace is badly needed in our world today. We know that many in our communities suffer from physical illnesses, but we must stay aware of those who suffer from spiritual illnesses too. Making a pilgrimage can help us do this. If you have never considered making one, think about it as an opportunity to "turbocharge" your spiritual life—both for yourself and for others. You don't have to go all the way to Lourdes to make a pilgrimage; a little online research will direct you to a number of shrines, abbeys, religious communities, and retreat houses in your area.

"I always make potato salad for potlucks. Do you think that's a sign of spiritual stagnation?"

Saints Preserve Us

Have you ever been driving down the highway when suddenly it starts to rain so heavily that you can hardly see in front of you? In Ireland, this type of rain is called "lashing rain" because it seems as if it is literally trying to lash you! During rainstorms like this, I (Julianne) feel a rush of gratitude for headlights, for the high and low beams that help me find my way safely through the rain.

There are times on our life's journey, too, when we undergo spiritual lashings during stormy times. Thank God for the saints, whose witness illuminates our way! Two especially bright lights are St. Francis of Assisi and St. Brigid of Ireland. As you read their stories below, inhale their spiritual wisdom. Then look for an opportunity to apply it in your own life—and especially in your classroom.

St. Francis of Assisi: Teach People What You Want Them to See

As catechists, we never stop learning, and the lives of the saints have much to teach us. From a legend associated with St. Francis of Assisi comes a practical and insightful catechetical principle that we should keep in mind when passing along the faith. According to the legend, St. Francis and a companion were walking through the busy square of Assisi one day. There were crowds of people in the marketplace talking, laughing, and going about their daily business. It was hot, noisy, and busy. In the midst of the commotion, St. Francis said to his companion, "Listen, can you hear the chirp of the cricket?" His friend responded, "Francis, how can you possibly hear a cricket in all this hustle and bustle?" With that, St. Francis threw a handful of coins into the air. The sound they made as they clanged and pinged against the cobblestones drew the attention of children and adults alike. The noise of the marketplace abruptly stopped as people scampered to gather up the coins.

Turning down a quiet side alley, St. Francis pointed to a small patch of grass nearby. "Listen carefully, my friend. Now can you hear the chirp of the cricket?" "Yes, yes, I can," his friend replied, absolutely astonished. "How could you possibly have heard this little creature above the noise of the crowd?" "People will listen to what their heart is attuned to," said Francis. "If you teach people to look for silence, they will find silence. If you teach people to look for God even among the noise and the busyness, they will find Him everywhere."

This lesson from St. Francis is a powerful reminder for us catechists to teach our students to look for God everywhere—especially in our daily lives—no matter how busy we become or how the noise of the world seeks to drown out his voice.

St. Brigid: Lift High the Cross

St. Brigid is one of Ireland's best-loved saints, and for good reason. Her entire life is a lesson in hospitality, warmth, and courage. Brigid was born to Dubhthach, a pagan chieftain, and Brocca, a Christian slave, in the early sixth century. She went on to found several monasteries in Ireland, most of them closely associated with the County of Kildare.

One of the most popular legends associated with Brigid is the story of the St. Brigid's Cross. St. Brigid, it is said, went to the bedside of a dying chieftain whose servants had summoned her in the hope that she could alleviate the suffering of the dying man. As she sat by his bedside, Brigid gathered the rushes from the floor and began to weave them into a cross. As she was weaving, Brigid shared with the chieftain why she loved her faith and explained the meaning of the cross in Christian life. So eloquent and spirited was Brigid in her storytelling that the old chieftain expressed a desire to be baptized before he passed away.

As a testament to Brigid's life and legacy, for 1400 years many Irish families keep the St. Brigid's cross displayed in their homes. Customarily, the crosses are made of rushes or straw and are woven on her feast day, February 1. They are placed over the doors of a house to ward off the threat of fire and evil.

As catechists, our best catechetical resources are our love for our faith, our witness to that faith, and our heartfelt understanding of the Scriptures. Like the tender, attentive ministries of Francis and Brigid, it is very often our own ministry of presence—our presence to our students, to those who are ill, to those who are difficult, and to those who are lonely—that speaks far more than we can ever say with words.

Saints on the Streets

In the song "Tears of the Saints," Christian artist Leeland declares that an emergency is happening in our midst: an emergency of suffering to which Christians must respond. He reminds us not only to teach the faith, but also to reach out with faith to the prodigal sons and daughters, the lonely and the lost in our midst as the saints have done before us. As Blessed Teresa tells us, "When a poor person dies of hunger, it has not happened because God did not take care of him or her. It has happened because neither you nor I wanted to give that person what he or she needed." This is a good reminder to us not just to teach our students about the lives of the saints, but also to encourage them to live as saints on the streets of our communities.

> **Everything the saints say and do is centered on Christ and points us in his direction.**
> —JAMES MARTIN, SJ
> *MY LIFE WITH THE SAINTS*

Questions for Reflection

> How would you describe your relationship with Mary? What story from the life of Mary do you treasure most? Why?

> What characteristic of Mary do you wish to more closely imitate?

> How does devotion to Mary bring you closer to Christ? What forms does your devotion to Mary take?

> How does Mary exemplify some or all of the characteristics of the spirituality of the catechist—openness to God, openness to the church, openness to the world, authenticity and consistency, and missionary zeal?
> What can you do in the days and weeks ahead to increase your devotion to Mary?
> Who is someone you know who has extraordinary devotion to Mary? How can you imitate him or her?
> Why do you think devotion to Mary is so important for catechists?
> Recall a time when your devotion to Mary helped you follow God's will.
> How can a deeper devotion to Mary impact the lives of those you teach?
> Consider family names. Are there recurring names in your family that reference a particular saint?
> What confirmation name did you choose? Why did you choose that name?
> Would you choose the same confirmation name today? Why or why not?
> Who are your favorite saints? Why?
> What are some ways you can deepen your love for the saints?
> Is there someone in your life whom you would describe as a "living saint"? For what reasons?

For Further Reflection

Reflect on these words of Pope Emeritus Benedict XVI's homily on the Solemnity of the Assumption of the Blessed Virgin Mary (August 15, 2006):

"And it is precisely by looking at Mary's face that we can see more clearly than in any other way the beauty, goodness and mercy of God. In her face we can truly perceive the divine light."

Spiritual Exercises

The following spiritual exercises were designed to deepen your devotion to Mary. Practice one or more of them, and then share the fruits of your experience with a fellow catechist.

> Take to heart—memorize with love—the words of Mary's *Magnificat* (also known as the Canticle of Mary), found in Luke 1:46-55. Learn two verses each day, and, at various times throughout the day, pray the

verses that you've learned. By the end of the week, you will know this beautiful prayer by heart.

> Pray the rosary every day for a week for the intentions of all the fellow catechists who have journeyed with you and for all those you teach. If you are new to the rosary, you can find good resources on the Internet to help you learn to pray it, such as those at www.loyolapress.com.

> A touching modern interpretation of the Nativity is "A Social Network Christmas" by Igniter Media, which you can find on YouTube. It tells the story of the Nativity as if Mary and Joseph were posting the news of Mary's pregnancy and the birth of Jesus on Facebook. The biblical details and emotions of these events are beautifully captured in a digital narrative format, and the music is especially uplifting and inspiring. Consider sharing this short video with your family, a friend, or your students, and using the clip to start discussion about the Nativity and societal attitudes today.

> Learn to pray the *Angelus*, a prayer based on Luke 1:26–27 that celebrates the incarnation of Christ and Mary's yes to God. Catholics traditionally pray the *Angelus* at 6:00 a.m., noon, and 6:00 p.m.

> *V. The Angel of the Lord declared unto Mary.*
> *R. And she conceived of the Holy Spirit.*
> > *Hail Mary . . .*
> *V. Behold the handmaid of the Lord.*
> *R. Be it done unto me according to thy word.*
> > *Hail Mary . . .*
> *V. And the Word was made flesh.*
> *R. And dwelt among us.*
> > *Hail Mary . . .*
> *V. Pray for us, O holy Mother of God.*
> *R. That we may be made worthy of the promises of Christ.*
>
> **Let us pray:** *Pour forth, we beseech thee, O Lord, thy grace into our hearts; that we, to whom the Incarnation of Christ, thy Son, was made known by the message of an angel, may by his Passion and Cross be brought to the glory of his Resurrection through the same Christ, our Lord.   Amen.*

> There are a number of excellent websites devoted to learning more about the saints and their lives. One unique way to deepen your appreciation of the saints is to try one of the many "patron saints generator" websites. With just a few clicks, you will be assigned a particular

saint and given background information, prayers, and other resources. Generating a patron saint for each of your students would be an excellent way of encouraging frequent reading and reflection on the lives of the saints.

> Read the following quotes and choose the one that most closely matches your sentiments about the saints. Consider why it does, then share it with a friend, post it on Facebook, or tweet it to your followers.

"[St. Thomas Aquinas] is medicine because he is an antidote. Indeed that is why the saint is often a martyr; he is mistaken for a poison because he is an antidote. He will generally be found restoring the world to sanity by exaggerating whatever the world neglects, which is by no means always the same element in every age. Yet each generation seeks its saint by instinct; and he is not what the people want, but rather what the people need."   —G. K. Chesterton

"Follow the saints, because those who follow them will become saints."   —Pope St. Clement I

"Don't call me a saint. I don't want to be dismissed so easily."   —Dorothy Day

"God creates out of nothing. Wonderful you say. Yes, to be sure, but he does what is still more wonderful: he makes saints out of sinners."   —Soren Kierkegaard

"Every saint has a past and every sinner has a future." —Oscar Wilde

---

What Catechists Are Saying about Devotion to Mary and the Saints

❝For all of us who have answered the call to be a catechist, this devotion is about following God's will. We all said 'yes' when asked to teach as Mary did when she was asked to be the Mother of God. Saying 'yes' is more difficult than saying 'no' and requires more work in the long run.   —*Mary Ann*

In my sixth grade class, I use Mary as a thread to explain and connect the Holy Days of Obligation. It keeps them from being separate bits of information, and it's a good way to also give the kids some understanding of the unique relationship between Jesus and his mother.   —*Christian*

Receiving a devotion to Mary when I entered the church two and a half years ago was an unexpected blessing. I was used to a "Jesus and me" spirituality: what a joy to realize that my new family (the communion of saints–both visible and invisible) had a mother! And as a mother myself, I deeply sense her undergirding presence strengthening and guiding me as I pray for my sons and my students. As a catechist, I learn from Mary that my willingness to listen and follow God's leading is more important than my words. 												*–Faith*

Since I was raised Catholic, Mary has always been with me . . . even during the years when I didn't feel like I was doing much practicing of my Catholicism. I honestly think I can give Mary the credit every time I have a "re-conversion." My most recent rediscovery of our faith a couple years ago was a commitment to start saying the rosary daily. I have kept that commitment, and for me, the incredible mysteries of the rosary have done so much to teach me about the life of Jesus. More than any other teaching, I think I love the mysteries. If I could spend a whole year teaching others about the life of Jesus, I think I would concentrate on nothing else but the mysteries of our beautiful rosary. The mysteries (and the Bible stories that they lead us to) have catechized me and continue to do so. The incredible Luminous Mysteries that were given to us by Pope John Paul II are something I have meditated on much more since becoming a catechist. I think these mysteries should be called the "catechist mysteries" as they all give great examples for us catechists to learn from and study. 		*–Ann*

Two thoughts stick out in my mind regarding our Blessed Mother. The first is that she offered tremendous support to me a few years back when my husband and I, along with a couple of his aunts, were helping my mother-in-law, who was terminally ill. There was one particular period when things were extremely bleak and I put out a heartfelt SOS to Mary. The answer to that prayer was different than what I expected, but much better than I ever imagined. The second reflection occurred just a couple of weeks ago when I was sitting in church before Mass started, looking at the stations of the cross. When I looked at the station of where "Jesus Meets His Mother," I was struck that even in his immense suffering, Jesus extended his compassionate love and care to his mother (and ultimately to us). 		*–Bernie*

Mary's immaculate heart shows us the love of the Sacred Heart of Christ with greater clarity! When one thinks of a mother, they usually think of a love so strong that words cannot describe it. Love is the only thing that lasts forever. Mary, as the Mother of Jesus, had the sweetest and most ardent love for Jesus of any human being. The love of this Mother's heart is so strong and powerful that God has favored Mary. He listens to her and highly respects her. It is this love of Mary that can help us to see more clearly how to live like her Son. She leads us to Christ! *—Eileen*

I had the opportunity to visit the village of Ars in France, where St. John Vianney spent his life as a parish priest. Because St. John Vianney is the patron saint of priests, I thought that I wouldn't be particularly drawn to him. However, as I strolled through the streets of Ars where St. John Vianney lived and worked, his life came alive for me. I sat in the coffee shop and ordered myself a large éclair (when in France, do as the French do!) and struck up a conversation with the waitress. She shared with me that the many thousands of people that visit Ars do get a sense of who St. John Vianney was, but that the villagers feel his presence in many subtle ways every day. His life and words seem to seep into their very being just by exposure to his life. I realized that the saints can touch us in unexpected ways, even those we expect least to connect with. Every saint has a story that we just need to familiarize ourselves with. *—Mary*

The night before the opening of hunting season our parish hosts a special Mass for the safety of those going into the woods. We ask St. Hubert, patron saint of hunters, to guide and watch over the hunters and have been doing it for about eight years now. Many children come to the Mass with their parents and always receive a special blessing for protection and safety. We also give out a holy medal of St. Hubert, which the hunters wear on their camouflage or blaze orange clothing. This Mass has become very popular and a good reminder for those present that the saints go with us in all of our activities, even into the woods! *—Mike*

My patron saint is the saint that I took as my confirmation name—St. Bernadette Soubirous. I have always loved the humility and courage that she displayed, even when she was interrogated by the authorities and made to feel small and ignorant. "Jesus is for me, honor, delight, heart and soul," she stated, and this is my favorite quote attributed to her. The name "Bernadette" means "brave as a bear," and she certainly lived up to her name! 🙟 *—Angela*

Chapter 7

Unpacking Your Backpack: Sharing Your Story of Faith

"Whether you were baptized as a child or joined the Church as an adult, you have a story of faith. Whether you sincerely live your faith in quiet or have a great public ministry, you have a story of faith. Whether you have a grade-school knowledge of the catechism or have a theological degree, you have a story of faith." —*Go and Make Disciples*, no. 6

All Good Things Must Come to an End

There comes a time when every backpacking adventure must end, and you must face the task of unpacking what you have taken with you on your journey. From your backpack, you pull out the essentials of your trip: flashlight, batteries, water bottle, utensils, matches, map, GPS, and other odds and ends. You empty your trusty backpack, scrub it down, and tuck it away for the next adventure. After you finish, you sit down, put your feet up, and take a moment to relax. You have successfully survived your backpacking adventure and unpacked your belongings.

Life Is Good!

But the best part of the adventure is yet to come. After the unpacking of your physical goods comes the unpacking of your stories about the trip. In the days, weeks, and months ahead, you will share memories, insights, and recollections related to the adventure with your friends and family. You find yourself reflecting on times of special significance and unpacking in your mind the overall experience of the trip. It can take some time to unfold the meaning of all that happened on a journey, and we often revisit special moments over and again, looking at them from different angles and seeing them in a different light as we ponder them in our hearts and share them with our friends.

Unpacking Our Spiritual Backpack

In our journey through life, certain experiences touch us at a very deep level. As catechists, we are called in a special way to "unpack" these experiences in the light of our faith. As we navigate the terrain of our lives, there are times when the road gets rocky and has more pitfalls and surprises than we would like. Other times, the terrain is flat, smooth, and easy to traverse. But through it all, God is with us.

It is in the sharing of our stories that communal bonds are strengthened, relationships are deepened, our faith is nourished, and God's movement in our lives is revealed.

Unpacking our story of faith is a necessary step for our own spiritual growth, of course, but it is also a wonderful way to evangelize and witness to our friends, family, and especially our students. Sharing our story of faith is a gift both for the story-teller and for the listener, for it is in the sharing of our stories that communal bonds are strengthened, relationships are deepened, our faith is nourished, and God's movement in our lives is revealed.

Once upon a Time

Countless beloved children's stories begin with the immortal words "Once upon a time." These words invite us to journey into someone else's world, taking us out of our own life and transporting us to another place and time. They invite us to take a risk, begin a new adventure, learn a new lesson, and walk a mile in the shoes of another. When I (Julianne) grab a book and say "Once upon a time," both my children perk up, for they know that we are about to be transported to another reality filled with adventure. As a result, we have each other's undivided attention for some time.

Storytelling is the oldest form of education and, in faith formation, we share the ultimate story of faith: the love story between God and his people. As catechists, we "echo" the stories from Scripture and the Tradition of the church, introducing them to new generations so that God's activity in the lives of his people will be revealed to them.

The Human Touch

In recent years, several Catholic publishers have produced appealing new catechetical programs consisting primarily of videos that promise to engage young people in a powerful experience of transformation. While it's true that our young people need to be more visually engaged in their catechetical formation, a troubling message is creeping into the catechetical community: all that's needed is someone to press the "play" button in order for young people to encounter Christ. Lured by ease of use, many catechetical leaders have come to the conclusion that they no longer need to invest so much time in forming catechists when all they really need are facilitators: warm bodies to activate the technology and keep students attentive. We view this as a dangerous trend. The *General Directory for Catechesis* reminds us of the following:

> No methodology, no matter how well tested, can dispense with *the person of the catechist* in every phase of the catechetical process. The charism given to him by the Spirit, a solid spirituality and transparent witness of life, constitutes the soul of every method. Only his own human and Christian qualities guarantee a good use of texts and other work instruments. (156, emphases ours)

Videos and technology in catechesis are much needed. Textbooks are crucial. However, *nothing* will ever replace the person of the catechist in faith formation and the ability of the catechist to share personal stories of faith.

Stories: Simply the Best!

If we catechists merely imparted facts and figures to our students without weaving a narrative, or story, the information we share would be far less effective and appealing. As an educational and catechetical technique, stories cannot be beat. From the Bible to Aesop's Fables, from *Lives of the Saints* to the Brothers Grimm, stories have long helped humans instill values, teach morals and ethics, and inspire others. Today, storytelling is finding new expression through digital and social media outlets such as Facebook, Vine, and Snapchat. Every tweet or status update is, in a sense, a mini-story, inviting readers into the life of the one who is sharing.

Stories help us organize and understand information, but, even more importantly, they have the capacity to touch the heart—both the story-teller's and the listener's. As we tell our stories, we discover areas of strength and weakness in our own character and opportunities for virtuous action and transformation. As they listen to our stories, our students will find parallels in their own lives. They will listen not only with their ears and minds, but with their hearts. As the old saying goes, "An arrow aimed at the head will not pierce the heart." As catechists, we seek not just to *form* and *inform* our students, but also to *transform* their lives. We have been given this awesome gift and privilege by virtue of our vocation as catechists.

> **The head does not hear anything until the heart has listened. The heart knows today what the head will understand tomorrow.**
> —James Stephens, Irish poet and philosopher

Stories: Fingerprints of the Heart

Just as valuable as teaching our students the Christian story is sharing our own personal journey of faith with them. In fact, the Christian story *is* our story. We have a place in it, and our students have a place in it—just as the people who heard Jesus' message sitting at his feet two thousand years ago did.

The Christian story is the story of God's great love for his people, our rejection of that love, and God's attempts to win us back over and over again. The Bible is a story of God's children distracting themselves from God's love with denials, greed, busyness, and addiction, and of others responding with faithfulness, trust, patience, and hope. Spanning two thousand years and featuring thousands of characters, the Christian story is expansive. It holds value and meaning regardless of the place, the culture, or the era of the person who hears it.

As catechists, we cannot expect students, especially children, to share their own story of faith with others and connect their story to the ultimate Christian story if they have not been taught how to do this. Likewise, as a church, we cannot expect our catechists or faith-sharing facilitators to tell effective stories from Scripture or about the saints and connect these stories to the events of their own lives if we have not given them these skills.

Each one of us has a story of faith as unique as our fingerprint. This story shapes our heart and soul and defines us. No two stories will ever be alike because every person sees the hand of God in his or her life differently. But in their own way, all our stories echo the paschal mystery. They speak of the life, death, and resurrection of Christ through our own experiences of brokenness and transformation.

Each one of us has a story of faith as unique as our fingerprint. This story shapes our heart and soul and defines us.

Unpacking Your Backpack: Sharing Your Story of Faith

Our culture bombards us with the "real" stories of other people through reality TV, which has undergone a tremendous explosion in recent years and emphasizes the sensational, the outrageous, and the outlandish. Our own stories may seem small and insignificant by comparison. You may wonder if you have a story at all, but you certainly do! With our own words we can paint the kind of picture that an hour of television will never offer. Your own story has the power to impact another's life and leave a lasting impression in ways that cannot be measured.

True, sharing our faith with others can seem like a daunting task—but it doesn't have to be! People are often far less interested in your knowledge of the Catholic faith than they are your experience of it. Outside of your actions, your story is the most powerful means by which you can evangelize. As long as you deliver your story in a heartfelt manner, you are unlikely to encounter yawning faces or closed ears.

WOW: Words of Witness

Words are powerful. They shape our worldview, our self-perception, and our perception of others. Consider the great lengths that people throughout history have undergone to preserve the written word. After the collapse of the Roman Empire, for example, European monks fled from the attacks of northern tribes who were burning their way through ancient libraries and destroying priceless manuscripts. At great risk, the monks secured the treasures of antiquity and took them to the British Isles for safe-keeping. A similar effort occurred during World War II, as Jewish people attempted to preserve the sacred texts of their faith from destruction at the hands of the Nazis. So powerful is the ability of stories and words to shape civilizations that their destruction and preservation are recurring motifs throughout history.

The Importance of Words

In the Bible, great importance is placed on the word because God and his Word are synonymous. As St. Jerome famously declared, "Ignorance of Scripture is ignorance of Christ." Consider the following Scripture quotes to help you reflect on the importance of words:

"In the beginning was the Word, and the Word was with God, and the Word was God."
                                                              —John 1:1

"But [Jesus] answered, 'It is written, "One does not live by bread alone, but by every word that comes from the mouth of God."'"
                                                              —Matthew 4:4

"Heaven and earth will pass away, but my words will not pass away."
                                                              —Matthew 24:35

"But what does it say? 'The word is near you, on your lips and in your heart,' (that is, the word of faith that we proclaim)."
                                                              —Romans 10:8

"So faith comes from what is heard, and what is heard comes through the word of Christ."
                                                              —Romans 10:17

Unpacking Your STORY of Faith

Knowing that we need to tell our story of faith and knowing how to tell our story of faith can be two very different things. Following are some of the essential elements of stories that speak from and to the heart and some strategies for shaping stories. To help you remember these elements, we offer the following acronym:

Structure
Trial
Openness
Redemption and Renewal
You-nique

✛ **Structure.** Every story needs structure. You can structure your story by highlighting the most significant experiences in your life.

> Name two or three times when you felt very clearly the presence of God before, during, or after an experience.

> Think of a passage or story from Scripture that speaks to or sheds light on each experience.

✚ **Trial.** Now that you have several specific experiences in mind to help structure your story of faith, focus on the aspect of "trial" in your story.

> How was your faith challenged in any of these experiences?

> Name two things that helped you persevere in this time of trial.

✚ **Openness.** At some point during your experience, darkness turned to light and you began to be more open and accepting of your situation.

> Identify the turning point. What happened?

> Who or what helped you become more open to God's presence?

✚ **Redemption and Renewal.** During every period of trial, there comes a time when we feel redeemed and renewed.

> Identify the moment you came to feel peace about your experience. How did this peace come?

> Which Person of the Trinity did you feel the presence of most powerfully through this experience? Why?

✚ **You-nique.** Your story of faith is unique, and yet at the same time it is universal.

> What makes your story unique?

> In what sense is your unique story universal? In other words, how is it part of the larger story of salvation revealed in Scripture?

> What do you believe to be the central message of your story?

> What impact are you hoping this story will have on others?

A good way to access your STORY is to write about it in a journal (see the Spiritual Exercises at the end of this chapter) or to sit with a spiritual companion or director and go through the above steps in prayerful sharing.

Sharing Our Story with Others

Ireland, where I (Julianne) was born, is famous for its culture of storytelling—and Irish stories are a delicious stew of legend, myth, magic, reality, and blarney! A common greeting when meeting someone is, "What's the story?" In other words, "What's going on?" or "Have I missed anything

A new catechist attended her first workshop on storytelling in catechesis. As people gathered and talked over refreshments, she heard someone call out, "Forty-two!" The whole room erupted in laughter. A little while later, another person called out, "Sixty-seven!" and this time a number of people were moved to tears. The catechist was intrigued and asked a fellow attendee what was going on. The other catechist responded, "Many of us have been coming to this storytelling workshop for years and we've told every story there is to tell, so finally we just assigned numbers to them. Now we shout out a number and everyone knows the story." The new catechist was fascinated and asked if she could try. The veteran catechist agreed, and after a slight hesitation the new catechist shouted out "Twenty-three!" There was no reaction at all, just the sound of crickets. The new catechist asked, "I don't get it. Why was there no reaction to my story?" The veteran catechist patted her on the shoulder and said, "We can tell you're a newcomer. You don't have the slightest idea how to tell a story."

interesting?" To the Irish, words are sacred and storytelling is revered as one of life's greatest gifts.

As Christian storytellers, we should share this passion and reverence for storytelling. We should also remember that everyone has a story to tell. If simple fishermen were able to do it, we can do likewise! Here are some additional tips that can help us as catechists share our stories of faith with those we teach.

- Identify stories from your life that resonate with the age group you are teaching. Children love to hear catechists recall stories from their own childhood. Teens need to know that you were also once a teenager who struggled with issues similar to those they struggle with. And adults need to hear stories that relate to work and family, not just "churchy" ones.

- Invite others to share their stories. Often, a story you tell will evoke similar ones in the minds of your listeners. While your story is unique, remember that it is also universal. Be sure that your

Keep It Simple

In his book *How to Share Your Faith with Anyone*, Terry Barber emphasizes that the first "law" of effective faith sharing is "keep it simple." If we get too theological or emotional, he points out, we might frighten away our listeners. Nevertheless, Barber adds, it is important for us to show genuine enthusiasm in sharing our faith story with others.

sharing is designed to help others find God in their lives, not just in yours.

➕ Don't overlook the ordinary. Too often, people feel compelled to emphasize the extraordinary in their stories—as though God's presence is revealed only in burning bushes and pillars of fire. As a result, listeners may conclude that their own lives or experiences of God are too ordinary to share. The key to faith sharing is precisely to help people recognize God in the ordinariness of their lives.

> **Always be ready to make your defense to anyone who demands from you an account of the hope that is in you; yet do it with gentleness and reverence.**
> —1 Peter 3:15–16

➕ Share only what is appropriate. We need not bare our souls to those we teach or share the intimate secrets of our lives with them. The purpose of our sharing is not spiritual therapy for ourselves. We simply need to share how we recognized God's presence in our lives, calling us to change and grow closer to him.

And They All Lived Happily Ever After

Many stories end with a "happily ever after." We, too, hope that by living in and through the Christian story, by following the commandments and growing in our love for Jesus Christ, we will have a share in the happiness that God has promised. The last book in the Bible, the Book of Revelation, tells us that at the end of time, "'He will wipe every tear from

Space between Words

One of the loveliest gifts the Irish monks gave the world was something quite simple that we often take for granted—the space between our words. Before the Middle Ages, written words had no spaces between them but instead ran together continuously on the page. However, the monks who were working in the scriptoriums of Ireland found it difficult to copy the intricate manuscripts without spaces between the words, and so began to separate them out.

The gift of space between words is not something that we should take for granted, especially when it comes to sharing our own faith stories. In the silent space between words, a depth of feeling and emotion may be conveyed. These spaces invite the listener or reader to enter the story and to pause and reflect on the meaning of what has come before.

their eyes. Death will be no more; mourning and crying and pain will be no more, for the first things have passed away.' And the one who was seated on the throne said, 'See, I am making all things new'" (Revelation 21:4–5). God is the author of life and, in a very real sense, the author of each of our stories. We are called to help write and tell the story. Every day is an opportunity to begin anew, for each day is a page and each week is a chapter in the story of God's love for us.

"God calls us to evangelism! The bank that holds our mortgage has mentioned it, too."

Questions for Reflection

> Who is the best storyteller you know? What qualities make him or her such a good storyteller? What can you learn from how this person tells stories?

> What are your favorite childhood stories? Why?

> What is your favorite Bible story? Why? What special meaning does it hold for you?
> Do you enjoy reading or hearing other people's stories? Why?
> What is your favorite Old Testament story? Why? What is your favorite New Testament story? Why?
> What stories have become important in your life?
> What stories do you find yourself sharing with others more than once?
> If you had to choose a title for the story of your life, what would it be?
> What stories from your life have you not shared with anyone? Why not? What would it take for you to be able to share one of them?
> The first time I felt God's presence in my life was . . .
> The first time I felt God speaking clearly to me was . . .

For Further Reflection

"We will first, like Jesus, join people in their daily concerns and walk side by side with them on the pathway of life. We will ask them questions and listen attentively as they speak of their joy, hope, grief, and anxiety. We will share with them the living word of God, which can touch their hearts and minds and unfold the deep meaning of their experience in the light of all that Jesus said and did. We will trust the capacity of prayer and sacrament to open their eyes to the presence and love of Christ. We will invite them to live and share this Good News in the world."

—Our Hearts Were Burning Within Us, no. 8–9, United States Conference of Catholic Bishops

Spiritual Exercises

The following exercises are designed to help you unpack your story of faith and share it with others. Practice one or more of them and then tell a fellow catechist what you learned.

> **Journaling.** Creative journaling is a good way to map out your story in a free-flowing way. Many devotees of this practice have a dedicated time for journaling each day. Consider combining your journaling time with your prayer time. As you pray, allow your mind to wander to important past or current events in your life. Note any themes or insights that come to mind. While writing, begin to sift through your observations to come up with a story of faith that you could share in three minutes, five minutes, or ten minutes.

> **Creating a Word Spiral or Word Cloud.** If you are a visual learner, a wonderful way to map your story of faith is through a word cloud or word spiral. Prepare your story of faith using the questions above or others of your own choosing. Then send your text to a word cloud website to generate a beautiful design made up of the words that appear most frequently in your story. This is also a simple and touching exercise to do with your students. Popular word cloud websites include www.wordle.net and www.wordlecreator.com.

> **Writing an Epitaph.** This strategy may strike some as a downer, but it is actually a great way to condense your story of faith and identify people and events that have played key roles. The following questions may be helpful as you write your epitaph.

   1. If you were to pass away, what would you want people to remember about your life?

   2. Identify three words that describe your life. Which events or relationships best illustrate these qualities?

   3. Which events in your life marked moments of passage or of closeness to God or others?

What Catechists Are Saying about Sharing Their Story of Faith

❝One of my classes focuses on each of the students sharing their story of faith. This class is made up of adult students from all ages and backgrounds. One of the students in my class was an older male who shared with the class that listening to the story of one of the youngest students in the room—a 19-year-old—had made a powerful impact upon him. The story was one of loss, sadness, and yet great hope. It was a story that this older gentleman knew well. What I learned through this experience is that a story is a story and reaches beyond age, culture, and background to touch people. It doesn't matter whether you are young or old. Everyone can be moved by someone else's story.   *–Wayne*

Nobody had ever asked me what my story of faith was, not in 54 years! One day a priest asked me why I was working for the church. I had plenty of reasons for my decision, but I could not answer his next question: Do you think your journey of faith led you to be here and now in this place? It was something I had never thought about before, but I began to think about this question and how true it was. Of course my faith journey has led me right to the place where God wanted me to be; I just didn't recognize it as such until I was asked to verbalize it. I guess the expression is true—God does not call the equipped, he equips the called!

—Justine

I think it is really important that we as Catholics share our faith with others. I started practicing how to share my story of faith with my family and closest friends. I learned a lot through that experience and ultimately it prepared me to share it with those that I didn't know as well. I never thought that I would be able to give a witness talk at my parish, but I did it! The support of the parish afterward was encouraging and heartfelt. I hope it inspired other people to talk about their life experiences through the lens of their faith. My advice to those who are thinking about how to share their story of faith is to put some time and effort into it. Be deliberate about what you decide to share in a spirit of prayer and don't get defensive when challenged.

—Brian

Biblical storytelling has entirely changed the way I encounter Scripture and subsequently it has changed my teaching at every step.

—Casey

I love hearing positive stories about faith because there is so much negativity in our society. It's nice to have positive stories in my head and heart to refer to when needed.

—Tamara

Everybody has a great story to tell! Storytelling is a powerful way to connect with others. There is a magic to storytelling: it's a way of creating a shared experience. The message that comes through in a faith story is, "If God can do this in my life, he can and is doing it in yours." Through the telling of personal stories, we can gain the trust of those we are teaching and we can inspire them. Stories make people think and they make people feel. Most of all, though, stories tap into the imagination, and that's incredibly important for faith formation. 🙶

—Matt

BIBLIOGRAPHY

Barber, Terry. *How to Share Your Faith with Anyone: A Practical Manual of Catholic Evangelization*. San Francisco: Ignatius Press, 2013.

Catechism of the Catholic Church. Second edition. Vatican: Libreria Editrice, Vaticana, 2000.

Evangelii Gaudium. 2013 (www.vatican.va).

Gaudium et Spes. Second Vatican Council, 1963 (www.vatican.va).

General Directory for Catechesis. Congregation for the Clergy, 1997.

Gilmore, James H. and B. Joseph Pine II. *Authenticity: What Consumers Really Want*. Cambridge, MA: Harvard Business School Press, 2007.

Go and Make Disciples: A National Plan and Strategy for Catholic Evangelization in the United States. Washington, DC: United States Conference of Catholic Bishops, 2002.

Guide for Catechists. Congregation for the Evangelization of Peoples, 1997 (www.vatican.va).

Kahnweiler, Jennifer B., Ph.D. *Quiet Influence: The Introvert's Guide to Making a Difference*. San Francisco: Berrett-Koehler Publishers, 2013.

Kruse, Kevin. "What Is Authentic Leadership?" *Forbes*, May 12, 2013.

Martin, James, SJ. *My Life with the Saints*. Chicago: Loyola Press, 2007.

Our Hearts Were Burning Within Us: A Pastoral Plan for Adult Faith Formation in the United States. Washington, DC: United States Conference of Catholic Bishops, 1999.

Paprocki, Joe. *7 Keys to Spiritual Wellness: Enriching Your Faith by Strengthening the Health of Your Soul*. Chicago: Loyola Press, 2012.

Robbins, Mike. *Be Yourself, Everyone Else is Already Taken: Transform Your Life with the Power of Authenticity*. San Francisco: Jossey-Bass, 2009.

Also by Joe Paprocki:
The Toolbox Series

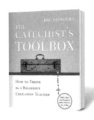

The Catechist's Toolbox
English | Paperback | 2451-5 | $9.95
Spanish | Paperback | 2767-7 | $9.95

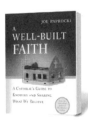

A Well-Built Faith
English | Paperback | 2757-8 | $9.95
Spanish | Paperback | 3299-2 | $9.95

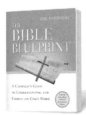

The Bible Blueprint
English | Paperback | 2898-8 | $9.95
Spanish | Paperback | 2858-2 | $9.95

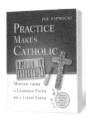

Practice Makes Catholic
English | Paperback | 3322-7 | $9.95

Beyond the Catechist's Toolbox
English | Paperback | 3829-1 | $7.95
Spanish | Paperback | 3882-6 | $7.95

TO ORDER: Call 800.621.1008 or visit **www.loyolapress.com/paprocki**.

Joe Paprocki's books are available as eBooks. Visit www.loyolapress.com to purchase these formats.

Also by Joe Paprocki

Living the Mass
How One Hour a Week Can Change Your Life

In *Living the Mass*, Joe Paprocki, DMin, and Fr. Dominic Grassi convincingly show how the one hour spent at Mass on Sunday can truly transform the other 167 hours of the week.

English | Paperback | 3614-3 | $13.95
Spanish | Paperback | 3758-4 | $13.95

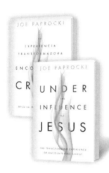

Under the Influence of Jesus
The Transforming Experience of Encountering Christ

In *Under the Influence of Jesus*, Joe Paprocki explains that by opening ourselves to encountering Christ, we can learn how to live the Gospel and be models of faith.

English | Paperback | 4050-8 | $15.95
Spanish | Paperback | 4211-3 | $15.95

7 Keys to Spiritual Wellness
Enriching Your Faith by Strengthening the Health of Your Soul

7 Keys to Spiritual Wellness provides a prescription for spiritual health based on the rich wisdom of Catholic Tradition.

English | Paperback | 3689-1 | $9.95